Original Sin

by Peter Gill

World Première Production

The Crucible, Sheffield

May 2002

Season Sponsor   Young People's Sponsor   Sheffield City Council   THE ARTS COUNCIL OF ENGLAND   Yorkshire Arts

the peter gill festival

When I first read Original Sin I was immediately excited by the possibility of seeing this magnificent new play on the Crucible stage. Having agreed to direct the play himself, Peter Gill presented us with a thrilling opportunity to introduce his work as both writer and director to a wider audience; this became the catalyst for embarking on a larger festival of his work.

In his plays, Peter Gill has inspired many of us over the years with his rich use of language and his strong poetic voice. His contribution to theatre in this country is immeasurable. As a director he has inspired an entire generation of actors and theatre practitioners to develop their craft.

Presenting a new play and a major retrospective of his work from the 1970s and 80s along with a programme of workshops, master-classes and exhibitions is amongst one of the most ambitious projects we have ever undertaken.

I am delighted to welcome him and an extraordinary cast and creative team to Sheffield

Michael Grandage
Associate Director

Theatre of the Year 2001
Barclays TMA Regional Theatre Awards

Best Actress, Victoria Hamilton, As You Like It
Barclays TMA Regional Theatre Awards

Best Director, Michael Grandage, As You Like It
Evening Standard Theatre Awards

Best Director, Michael Grandage, As You Like It
The Critics' Circle Award

As You Like It
The South Bank Show Award For Theatre

Financial Times/Arts & Business Awards
(shortlisted)

Victoria Hamilton in
As You Like It
2000

Photograph: Simon Warner

Original Sin

by Peter Gill

Director	Peter Gill
Designer	Alison Chitty
Assistant Designer	Jessica Curtis
Lighting Designer	Hartley T A Kemp
Composer	Terry Davies
Casting Director	Julia Horan
Assistant Director	Nikolai Foster
Stage Manager	Di Stalker
Deputy Stage Manager	Kath Bools
Assistant Stage Manager	Kim Lewis

Literal translations of Wedekind's 'Earth Spirit' and 'Pandora's Box' by D. C. Holmes.

Original Sin

by Peter Gill

Cast in order of speaking:

Slavin, an itinerant	John Normington
Leopold Southerndown, a newspaper proprietor	Michael Byrne
Eugene Black, a painter	Adam James
Dr. Edwin Goulderie, a physician	Paul Imbusch
Angel	Andrew Scott
Arthur Southerndown, Southerndown's son, a playwright and theatre director	Steve John Shepherd
Hugo Anstruther, a schoolboy	Andrew Fallaize
Stage Manager } theatre workers	Robert Styles
Dresser	Barry Howard
Buller, a strongman	David Kennedy
Lord Henry Wantage, a follower of Angel	Richard Cant
Frederick, a footman	Michael Shaeffer
The Marchese di Casti Piani, a white slaver	Clive Arrindell
Weil, a banker	Richard Cant
Phillipeau, a journalist	Robert Styles
Baron St. Eglise, one of Angel's guests	Paul Imbusch
August, his protégée	Andrew Fallaize
Baptiste } other guests	Michael Shaeffer
Hippolyte	David Carr
Bob, a footman	Paul Child
Mr. Tompkins	Barry Howard
Euba } Angel's clients	David Carr
Jack	Michael Shaeffer

Other parts played by the company.

The action of the play takes place in London and Paris in the 1890's.

biographies

CLIVE ARRINDELL
Marchese di Casti Piani

Trained: Central School of Speech and Drama
Theatre: Rep work includes York, Worcester. Many theatre credits including Love's Labour's Lost, The Winter's Tale, A Midsummer Night's Dream and title role in Henry V (Regents Park); Henry V, Twelfth Night and Much Ado About Nothing (Royal Exchange, Manchester) The Night Of The Burning Pestle (RSC at The Aldwych Theatre); many Royal Theatre credits including: Richard II,The Mayor Of Zalemea, Le Malade Imaginaire, Lorenzaccio and The Spanish Tragedy. Also A Midsummer Night's Dream (Young Vic), Richard II & III with Derek Jacobi in the title role in Richard III at Ludlow Festival; Double Indemnity (Theatr Clwyd); Much Ado About Nothing (USA tour for ACTER); For Michael Bogdanov: Beowulf, As You Like It and Antony and Cleopatra (English Shakespeare Company), A Christmas Carol (Birmingham Rep).
Television includes: A Mind To Kill; The Scarlet And Black; Dream Team; Making News; Poor Little Rich Girl; Daphne Laureola with Laurence Olivier for Granada; Cats Eyes; Design for Living.
Film: Turbulence; Columbus, The Sleeping Beauties

MICHAEL BYRNE
Leopold Southerndown

Theatre includes:
Filumena for The Peter Hall Company; Phaedre;

Kafka's Dick; Hamlet; The Duchess Of Malfi and Man And Superman. New World Order, Double Dealer, Lulu (Royal Court); Death And The Maiden (Royal Court and Duke Of York's); Julius Caesar (Riverside Studios); Close Of Play, Undiscovered Country, Double Dealer, Bond Honoured, Black Comedy, Trelawney Of The Wells, Much Ado About Nothing, Entertaining Strangers (Royal National Theatre).
Television includes: Sunday; Mists Of Avalon; Holocaust On Trial; The Vice; Imogen's Face; Hornblower; Deadly Voyage; No Bananas; Sharpe; Between The Lines; The Orchid House; The Happy Valley; Smiley's People; Richard III and Henry VI.
Film includes: to be released: Martin Scorcese's Gangs Of New York; Sum Of All Fears and Musketeers. Other credits include: Proof Of Life; Tomorrow Never Dies; The Saint; Braveheart; Nostradamus; Indiana Jones (III); The Long Good Friday; A Bridge Too Far; The Eagle Has Landed.

RICHARD CANT
Lord Henry Wantage

Theatre: She Stoops To Conquer (New Kent Opera); The Country Wife (Sheffield); Pera Palas (Gate/RNT Studio); Other People (Royal Court); Angels In America (Manchester Library); Hamlet, Cymbeline, Much Ado About Nothing (RSC); The Canterbury Tales (Garrick Theatre); As You Like It (Cheek by Jowl); Waterland (Shaw Theatre).
Television: The Way We Live Now; Shackleton; In A Land Of Plenty; Sunburn; Midsomer Murders; This Life; Gimme, Gimme, Gimme.
Film: The Lawless Heart.

DAVID CARR
Euba/Hippolyte

Theatre: credits include Macbeth, Deadmeat, Wicked Gamers and Comedy Of Errors (West Yorkshire Playhouse); Zebra Crossing Two, Resurrections, Arawak Gold and Antony and Cleopatra (Talawa Theatre Company); Weathering The Storm (Lyric Hammersmith), King of France in King Lear (Crucible Theatre); Tybalt and Friar in Romeo and Juliet (USA tour); Pow (Paines Plough); Zumbi (Stratford East and tour); Henry V and Puck in A Midsummer Night's Dream (Royal National Theatre); Jake Malcolm in The Carver Chair (Contact, Manchester); Trouble In Mind (Tricycle Theatre); Goya (BAC); The Emperor Jones (Anglo/American Theatre Company).
Television: credits include John Wilson and Worsley in The Bill (Thames); Sergeant Daley in Soldier Soldier (Carlton); Casualty (BBC); Michael Heathfield in A Touch Of Frost (Yorkshire Television).
Radio: Freefall by Debbie Green (BBC Radio).

PAUL CHILD
Bob

Theatre: includes An Inspector Calls (Aldwych Theatre); Oliver! (Palladium).
Television: includes My Hero; Hidden City; The Bill; Family Affairs; Totally Mad; The Worst Witch (three series);

Maisie Raine; Men Behaving Badly; My Dead Buddy; Johnny And The Dead; The Famous Five (two series).

ANDREW FALLAIZE
Hugo Anstruther/August

Theatre: The Prince Of Homburg (RSC/Lyric, Hammersmith); House/Garden (Royal National Theatre); The School For Wives (BAC).
Television/Film: Who Can I Turn To?
Radio/Audio: The Merry Wives Of Windsor; How The White King Died.

BARRY HOWARD
Dresser/Weil/Mr Tomkins

Theatre: Dozens of pantomimes; Scrooge; Hard Fruit (Royal Court); No Sex, Please We're British; One For The Pot; Pirates Of Penzance; Rocky Horror Show; Bedful Of Foreigners; Witness For The Prosecution; Run For Your Wife; Nearest And Dearest; His Favourite Family; Oliver!; Cabaret; Winnie; Wizard Of Oz; The Bed; Boeing Boeing; What A Racket; Out Of Order; And Then There Were None.
Television: Hi-de-Hi; Dad; Harry Hill; House Of Windsor; You Rang M'Lord.
Radio: The Gamester; R.T.E.

ADAM JAMES
Black

Training: Guildhall 1993 - 1996.
Theatre: Time And The Conways, Snake In Fridge, King Lear (Royal Exchange); The Glass Menagerie (Minerva); Chimes At Midnight (Chichester); Poor Superman - nominated for Best Newcomer in Manchester Evening News Award (Royal Exchange); Unseen Hand, Lone Stars And Private Wars (Bristol Old Vic); A View From The Bridge (Theatre Royal, York); Tamburlaine The Great (RSC); Coriolanus (NYT).
Television: Table 12 - After Hours (BBC); The Lost Battalion; Murder On The Orient Express; Band Of Brothers; I Saw You (Granada); Tenth Kingdom; Let Them Eat Cake (BBC); Silent Witness (BBC); Island (Channel TV); Sharpe's Regiment (Central); Cold Lazarus (Channel 4).
Film: High Heels And Low Life; It's Not You It's Me; Three Blind Mice; Life Of The Party; Gregory's 2 Girls; Forbidden Territory.
Radio: The Nature Of Fighting, Selling Imorality.

PAUL IMBUSCH
Dr. Goulderic/Baron St. Eglise

Theatre: Paul started out as a trained singer. Has been both a Royal National Theatre and Royal Shakespeare Company player. He has performed at the Royal Exchange Manchester, Bristol, Birmingham, and other principal theatre venues; plus tours with English Touring Theatre

and others. Most recently he was seen in Peter Gill's production of Luther at the Royal National Theatre.
Television: A large number of television appearances include The Bill and other popular series.
Film: include Monsignor Quixote; Personal Services; Sporting Club Dinner and Caleb Williams.

DAVID KENNEDY
Buller

Training: Webber Douglas
Theatre: No Sweat (Birmingham Repertory Theatre); Meat (Theatre Royal, Plymouth); Tender, Hushabye Mountain - nominated for Best Actor Award, Manchester Evening News (Hampstead Theatre); Richard III, A View From The Bridge (Leicester Haymarket); Coriolanus, Messiah for Steven Berkoff); Death Of A Salesman (Royal National Theatre); Dealer's Choice (Vaudeville Theatre); Blue Remembered Hills (Cheltenham, Everyman); The Hairy Ape (Bristol Old Vic).
Television: Ultimate Force; Waking The Dead; London's Burning; Without Motive; Big Smoke; Trial And Retribution; Dream Team; Supply And Demand; Strange But True; Nelson's Column; Moving Story; 99 To 1; Alexei Sayle Show; Soldier Soldier; Pie In The Sky; The Bill.
Film: Reign Of Fire; Down; The Biographer; Shiner; Shooters; Gangster No 1; Dreaming of Joseph Lees; Love Is The Devil; Nil By Mouth; The Fifth Element; Mary Shelley's Frankenstein.
Radio: Central 822 and Michael And Me (BBC Radio 4).

JOHN NORMINGTON
Slavin

Training: Northern School of Music.
Theatre: includes RSC, Royal National Theatre and West End. Homecoming; Wars Of The Roses; Guys And Dolls; Danton's Death, The Fool and As You Like It - directed by Peter Gill; Master Builder; The Mysteries; The Winter's Tale; The Good Hope.
Television: Inspector Morse; The Bill; Hercule Poirot; Dr Who; Casualty; Preston Front.
Radio: Jude The Obscure; Amadeus.
Film: Private Function; Stardust; Roller Ball; The Medusa Touch.

ANDREW SCOTT
Angel

Theatre: The Cavalcaders (Tricycle); Crave (Royal Court); The Coming World (Soho Theatre); The Secret Fall Of Constance Wilde (Abbey Theatre/ Barbican, RSC); Dublin Carol (Old Vic/Royal Court Downstairs); Lonesome West (Druid Theatre Co); Long Days Journey Into Night - nominated best supporting actor, Irish Times Theatre Award i98 (The Gate, Dublin); The Marriage Of Figaro, A Woman of No Importance, Six Characters In Search Of An Author (Abbey Theatre); Andrew was awarded Spirit of Life, Irish Independent Actor Of The Year '98.
Television: Band of Brothers; The American; Budgie; Longitude (Granada)
Film: Cigarette Girl (BBC); Nora; Saving

Private Ryan; Sweetie Barrett; Miracle At Midnight; Drinking Crude; Korea.

MICHAEL SHAEFFER
Jack, Baptiste, Frederick

Theatre: Macbeth (Southwark Playhouse); Thomas in The Beautiful Game (Cambridge Theatre); Annas in Jesus Christ Superstar (national tour); Billy Bibbet in One Flew Over The Cuckoo's Nest (ICA Theatre, London); Mr Jackson in Live Like Pigs and Paris in Romeo and Juliet (The Barn Theatre); Publius in Titus Andronicus (Cambridge Arts); Ariel in The Tempest (Saffron Shakespeare Festival); Dennis Potts in Dancing In The Street (national tour); Mickey Thompson in Glad All Over (national tour); Madness (workshop for Tiger Aspect); Rodgers and Hart (workshop).
Television: EastEnders (BBC); World In Arms (Channel 4); Navvies.
Film: The Sandwich; Jesus Christ Superstar.

STEVE JOHN SHEPHERD
Arthur

Theatre: Dangerous Corner; Twelfth Night.
Television: Choice Chillers - The Lovegods (BBC); The Knock (LWT); Forgive And Forget (Scottish TV); An Unsuitable Job For A Woman; Maisie Raine (Series I & II); This Life (Series I & II - BBC); The One That Got Away (LWT); Christmas (Channel 4).
Film: Star Wars Episode II; Now You See Her; Me Without You; From Hell; Greenwich Mean Time; Virtual Sexuality; RPM; I Want You.

ROBERT STYLES
Stage Manager/
Phillipeau

Trained: Arts Educational
School.
Theatre: A Patriot For Me
(RSC); Chicago (English
Speaking Theatre,
Frankfurt); What The
Butler Saw (Coventry and
York); The Importance Of
Being Earnest and Lend
Me A Tenor (York); Wind
In The Willows
(Birmingham Rep and
Theatr Clwyd); Crime Of
The Century and A
Christmas Carol
(Birmingham Rep); A
Midsummer Night's
Dream, Twelfth Night and
The Swaggerer (Open Air
Theatre, Regent's Park);
Breaking The Code and
Consent (Basingstoke).
Television: EastEnders;
B.U.G.S.; Vanity Fair
(BBC).
Film: Cromwell And
Fairfax; Hamlet.
Radio: Jim Davis
(BBC Radio 4).

PETER GILL
Playwright/Director

Theatre includes: The
York Realist (English
Touring Theatre, Royal
Court and Strand
Theatres); for the RNT:
Luther, A Month In The
Country, Much Ado About Nothing,
Danton's Death, Major
Barbara, Tales From
Hollywood, Small
Change, Kick For Touch,
Antigone, Venice
Preserv'd, Fool For Love,
The Murderers, As I Lay
Dying, A Twist Of Lemon,
In the Blue, Bouncing, Up
For None, The Garden Of
England, Show Songs,
Mean Tears, Mrs Klein,
Juno And The Paycock,
Cardiff East and Scrape
Off The Black; for the
Royal Court: A Collier's
Friday Night, The Local
Stigmatic, The Ruffian On
The Stair, A Provincial
Life, A Soldier's Fortune,
The Daughter-in-Law, The
Widowing Of Mrs
Holroyd, Life Price, The
Sleepers Den, Over
Gardens Out, The
Duchess Of Malfi, Crete
and Sergeant Pepper, The
Merry-Go-Round, The
Fool and Small Change;
for the Riverside Studios:
The Cherry Orchard, The
Changeling, Measure For
Measure, Julius Caesar;
for the RSC: Twelfth
Night, New England and
A Patriot For Me; at the
Queen Elizabeth Hall:
Bow Down and Down By
The Greenwood Side; for
Opera North: The
Marriage Of Figaro; for
the Lyric, Hammersmith:
The Way Of The World;
for Field Day: Uncle
Vanya; for the Almeida:
Tongue Of A Bird and
Certain Young Men; for
the New Ambassadors:
Speed-The-Plow.
Plays include: The
Sleepers Den, Over
Gardens Out, Small
Change, Kick For Touch,
In The Blue, Mean Tears,
Cardiff East, Certain
Young Men, Friendly Fire,
The York Realist, Original
Sin.
Adaptations and
Versions: A Provincial
Life, The Merry-Go-
Round, The Cherry
Orchard, Touch And Go,
As I Lay Dying, The
Seagull.

ALISON CHITTY
Designer

Training: St Martin's
School of Art and Central
School of Art and Design.
Theatre work includes:
Ecstasy and Uncle Vanya
(Hampstead Theatre);
Measure For Measure
and Julius Caesar
(Riverside Studios); A
Month In The Country,
Don Juan, Danton's
Death, Venice Preserv'd
(British Drama Award),
Tales From Hollywood,
Fool For Love (West End),
Antony And Cleopatra,
The Late Shakespeares
and Remembrance Of
Things Past (Olivier
Award for Best Costume
Designer) and Luther (all
Royal National Theatre);
Tartuffe, Volpone and
Hamlet (RSC); Orpheus
Descending (Haymarket
and Broadway).
Opera includes: New
Year (Houston and
Glyndebourne); Gawain
and Arianna (ROH);
Jenufa (Dallas); Billy Budd
(Geneva, Paris, LA, ROH -
Olivier Award);
Khovanschina (ENO -
Olivier Award);
Meistersinger
(Copenhagen); Turandot
(Paris); The Flying
Dutchman and Julius
Caesar (Bordeaux);
Tristan And Isolde (Seattle
and Chicago); Otello
(Munich); Dialogues Of
The Carmelites (Santa
Fe); Aida (Geneva) and
The Last Supper (Berlin
and Glyndebourne).
Film work includes: Mike
Leigh's Life is Sweet;
Naked and Secrets And
Lies (Palm D'Or, Cannes).
She is Director of Motley
Theatre Design Course.

JESSICA CURTIS
Assistant Designer

Training: Motley Theatre
Design Course.
Theatre: The Wizard of Oz
(West Yorkshire
Playhouse); Macbeth (Nor
Jyske Opera); Dangerous
Corner (West Yorkshire
Playhouse and The
Garrick Theatre); A
Clandestine Marriage
(The Watermill Theatre);
The Europeans (The
British American Drama
Academy); Arms and The
Man (Exeter and The
Mercury Theatre,
Colchester);I Three
French Operas (Guildhall
School of Music and
Drama); Orpheus in The
Underworld (Den Ny
Opera, Denmark); Second
to Last in The Sack Race
(The New Victoria
Theatre, Stoke); The Rise
and Fall of Little Voice
(Salisbury Playhouse);
Local Boy (Hampstead
Theatre); Dangerous
Corner (Palace Theatre,
Watford); Sugar Sugar
(The Bush Theatre); A
Winter's Tale (The
National Theatre Studio);
218: Underground
(National Youth Theatre);
The Rakes Progress and
Don Giovanni (Royal
Scottish Academy of
Music and Drama); A
Rakes Progress (British
Youth Opera); Vanessa
(Trinity College of Music).
Film: I Just Want To Kiss
You (BBC 2 Brief
Encounters); You Shall
Have A Fishy (Open Eye
Productions).

biographies

HARTLEY T A KEMP
Lighting Designer

Theatre: work with Peter Gill includes The York Realist (English Touring Theatre/Royal Court), Certain Young Men and Tongue Of A Bird (Almeida). Work for the Crucible, Sheffield includes Don Juan, The Country Wife, As You Like It, A View From The Bridge, Twelfth Night and Queueing For Everest. Other recent work includes The Merchant Of Venice (RSC UK and international tour); Passion Play and Good (Donmar Warehouse); The Doctor's Dilemma (Almeida and UK tour); 50 Revolutions (Oxford Stage Company, Whitehall Theatre); No Sweat (Birmingham Rep); Dealer's Choice (Theatre Clywd and West Yorkshire Playhouse); Faith (Royal Court Upstairs); The Disputation and The Queen Of Spades And I (Pluto Productions, New End); Thieves Like Us, In The Jungle Of Cities, Rosmersholm and Seascape With Sharks And Dancer (Southwark Playhouse); When Did You Last See Your Mother? (BAC).
Opera: recent credits include: Mary Seacole (Gynyame, Royal Opera House Linbury Studio); Oreste and Oresteia (English Bach Festival Opera, Royal Opera House Linbury Studio); Iris (Opera Holland Park); M Butterfly, Martha, The Barber Of Seville, La Sonnamubula and Carmen (Castleward Opera, Castleward and Belfast); Die Fledermaus (London City Opera, Chichester Festival Theatre and tour); and The Marriage Of Figaro (QEH and tour).
Musicals: recent work includes: Show Boat and West Side Story (Tiroler Landestheater,

Innsbruck); Dorian (Arts Theatre); Jesus Christ Superstar (Theatre Royal, Hanley); Assassins and Sweet Lorraine (Old Fire Station, Oxford); and The Happy Prince (tour). Hartley is also Artistic Director of C venues at the Edinburgh Festival.

TERRY DAVIES
Composer

Terry is a composer and conductor whose credits include films, theatre and TV for many countries around the world. His dance piece The Car Man was winner of the Evening Standard Award for Best Musical Event 2000.
Theatre compositions include: Luther, The Rise And Fall Of Little Voice, The Misanthrope, Neaptide, The Festival Of New Plays, Antigone and Tales From Hollywood (Royal National Theatre); Alice In Wonderland, A Patriot For Me, New England and Coriolanus (RSC); Life After George (The Duchess Theatre); Lady In The Van (Birmingham Rep); Speed The Plow (Ambassadors and Duke of York's); Romeo And Juliet, As You Like It, Love's Labour's Lost, Much Ado About Nothing, Twelfth Night and A Midsummer Night's Dream (Regent's Park Theatre). The York Realist, Hushabye Mountain and The School For Scandal (English Touring Theatre); Alarms And Excursions (Gielgud Theatre); Tongue Of A Bird (Almeida Theatre); The Snow Queen (Theatr Clwyd); Uncle Vanya (Field Day); The Way Of The World (Lyric, Hammersmith) and Richard III (Icelandic National Theatre). Terry has written two musicals: Kes (music and lyrics for Octogon Theatre, Bolton and Theatre Royal, York)

and The Birds (Istanbul City Theatre).
Television: Conductor and/or orchestrator credits include: The Inspector Lynley Mysteries; Flesh And Blood; Sinners; Dalziel and Pascoe; Shackleton; Crime And Punishment; Bloody Sunday; Perfect Strangers (BAFTA nominated score); Jason and the Argonauts; Super Human; The Mayor Of Casterbridge; Turn Of The Screw; All The King's Men; Shooting The Past (winner Prix Italia, 1999); Our Mutual Friend and Deacon Brodie.
Film: Terry has orchestrated and conducted the scores for Doctor Sleep; The Lawless Heart; The Sleeping Dictionary; Born Romantic; A Midsummer Night's Dream (Michelle Pfeiffer and Kevin Kline version); The War Zone; Perdita Durango; Cousin Bette and Photographing Fairies and orchestrated The Parole Officer. He also conducted the music for The House Of Mirth; Some Voices; About Adam; The Suicide Club; The Last Yellow; With Or Without You; Shakespeare In Love (co-conductor - Oscar-winning score); The Debt Collector and Divorcing Jack.

NIKOLAI FOSTER
Assistant Director

Nikolai trained at Drama Centre London, graduating in July 2001. Work as assistant director whilst training included The Importance of Being Earnest (Queens Theatre Hornchurch), The Rendezvous (Cochrane Theatre), The Merchant Of Venice, Middleton's Women, Beware Women and Koltes' Roberto Zucco (all Drama Centre).

He comes to the Crucible

on the Channel Four Theatre Director Scheme, where he has assisted Michael Grandage on Richard III and Don Juan, Angus Jackson on Mamet's Sexual Perversity In Chicago and The Shawl, Fiona Laird on High Society (on which he was also resident director) and Erica Whyman on Pinter's The Birthday Party.

about sheffield theatres

Sheffield Theatres is the largest theatre complex outside London, offering a wide range of performances from drama to dance, comedy to musicals.

The Crucible Theatre, built in 1971 houses a thrust stage and is the main producing venue in the complex. Recently awarded the Barclays Theatre of the Year Award, productions have included Kenneth Branagh in Richard III directed by Michael Grandage, The Birthday Party directed by Erica Whyman, High Society directed by Fiona Laird, Sexual Perversity In Chicago and The Shawl directed by Angus Jackson, Tom Hollander in Don Juan directed by Michael Grandage, The Arbor directed by Anna Mackmin, Joseph Fiennes in Edward II and Victoria Hamilton in As You Like It both directed by Michael Grandage.

The Lyceum Theatre, built in 1897, receives the country's top touring theatre including visits by the Royal National Theatre, The Royal Shakespeare Company, Opera North, Northern Ballet Theatre and hit shows from the West End.

The Studio Theatre, a flexible 'black box' space plays host to smaller touring companies, contemporary dance and is home to the world famous Lindsays and Friends Chamber Music Festivals.

Joseph Fiennes in
Edward II
2001

Kenneth Branagh in
Richard III
2002

Photographs: Ivan Kyncl

the square circle

Sheffield Theatres operates a flexible membership scheme that not only rewards frequent theatre goers but also encourages young first-time attenders:

- A range of membership levels to suit every need and budget
- Generous ticket discounts
- Priority booking
- Talks, tours and opportunities to meet the acting companies and production teams
- Regular newsletter and brochure mailings
- Members' Hotline

For further information contact Alison Moore:
tel: 0114 249 6007/email: alison@sheffieldtheatres.co.uk.

education

Sheffield Theatres Education Programme actively engages people in the work of the Theatre through a varied and challenging programme of activities and events. It is designed for all those who wish to understand and discover more about the process of creating theatre. The Education programme reflects the rich cultural diversity of its community and encourages access and inclusion. It includes:

- theatre in schools and community venues
- youth theatre and projects with young people
- special education projects with the early years, schools and colleges, and the community
- education programmes supporting sheffield theatres productions including talks, a range of workshops, and resource packs
- backstage tours and specialist tours
- work experience and student placements
- training and development programme for teachers and education workers.

For further information contact Sue Burley, Education Administrator on 0114 249 5999.

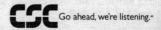

**Sheffield
Assay Office**

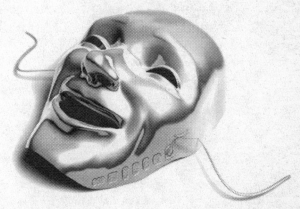

There's no drama
with British Hallmarks

THE BRITISH HALLMARK - PROTECTING THE CONSUMER FOR OVER 700 YEARS

British Hallmarking dates back 700 years and represents the earliest form of consumer protection. The Hallmark shows that precious metal articles have been independently tested by an Assay Office and guarantees that the article conforms to a specified legal standard of purity. The Hallmark consists of three compulsory symbols: a sponsor's mark, the fineness number and the Assay Office mark. Unless specifically exempted, all gold, silver and platinum articles offered for sale must be Hallmarked. There may be additional voluntary marks, *eg* a date letter, a fineness symbol, a common control mark. The Hallmarking Act permits other European Area Hallmarks and standards of fineness.

Sponsor	Millesimal Number	Assay Office	Fineness Symbol	Date Letter	Common	

Sponsor
The registered mark of the maker or sponsor of the piece

Millesimal Number
Indicates the precious metal content. The shape of the shield identifies the metal as gold, silver or platinum

Assay Office
The mark of the Assay Office where the piece was tested

Fineness Symbol
A traditional symbol denoting one of the older precious metal finenesses

Date Letter
A letter representing the year in which the piece was hallmarked

Common Control Mark
Indicates countries which are signatories to the International Convention on Hallmarking

A special mark for 2002 to commemorate HM Queen's Golden Jubilee

**Assay Master: Ashley Carson, PO Box 187, 137 Portobello Street, Sheffield, S1 4DS
Tel: 0114 275 5111 Fax: 0114 275 6473
carsona@assayoffice.co.uk**

Peter Gill
Original Sin

after Frank Wedekind

faber and faber

First published in 2002
by Faber and Faber Limited
3 Queen Square London WC1N 3AU
Published in the United States by Faber and Faber Inc.
an affiliate of Farrar, Straus and Giroux LLC, New York

Typeset by Country Setting, Kingsdown, Kent CT14 8ES
Printed in England by Mackays of Chatham plc, Chatham, Kent

A CIP record for this book is available
from the British Library

0-571-21243-3

2 4 6 8 10 9 7 5 3 1

To John, Deirdre, Bill and Alison

Characters

Slavin
an itinerant

Leopold Southerndown
a newspaper proprietor

Eugene Black
a painter

Dr Edwin Goulderie
a physician

Angel

Arthur Southerndown
Southerndown's son, a playwright
and theatre director

Hugo Anstruther
a schoolboy

Stage Manager *and* **Dresser**
theatre workers

Buller
a strong-man

Lord Henry Wantage
a follower of Angel

Frederick
a footman

The Marchese di Casti Piani
a white slaver

Weil
a banker

Phillipeau
a journalist

Baron St Eglise
one of Angel's guests

August
his protégé

Baptiste, Hippolyte
other guests

Bob
a footman

Policemen

Mr Tomkins, Euba, Jack
Angel's clients

*The action of the play takes place
in London and Paris in the 1890s*

Enter Slavin, singing.

Slavin

What's the use of kicking up a row
If there ain't no work about?
If you can't get a job you can rest in bed
Till the schoolkids all come out.
If you can't get work you can't get the sack.
That's an argument that's sensible and sound.
Lay your head back on yer piller
And read yer *Daily Mirrer*
And wait till the work comes round.

(*to the audience*) Anyone who says he can't make a living is a liar. As I am here to show. I've managed. I've managed. It's a matter of priorities and motivation. But that's not to be the thrust of things. No. No. No. Right then. London. 1890. 1890s London. That'll mean something to you. But perhaps I should re-emphasise what you might think is obvious. Fog, for example. Cab horses, for instance. Street lamps lit by gas. London squares and tenement dwellings. East and West. The poor and the destitute, the rich and the powerful. All that. And you'll have thought perhaps of extravagant opulence and gilded youth. The beautiful and the damned. Yes.

Noise of monkeys chattering and screaming.
Parakeets. A wolf howling. Big cats snarling.

What's that?

Similar noises.

7

Oh yes. The street cries of London. Yes. This is to be about the world of men. Of power and cash and the force that seems to drive it all. And if I say, artist and studio and that's where we'll begin, you'll think perhaps of the embankment alongside the river in the mist and the barges and factories and the oily water lapping against the wharves and the bridges dim in the evening light and the little unexploited streets and the north-facing windows and the cold. See where I fit into all this. If I do.

ONE

London. An artist's studio. Prominent, a woman's evening dress on a stand. Unaffected but sumptuous. Near it on an easel, the unfinished portrait of a young man. Leopold Southerndown talking to Eugene Black.

Southerndown (*handing the artist a pair of women's evening gloves*) And these perhaps.

Black Yes.

Southerndown No jewels, I think.

Black No.

Southerndown Flowers? Perhaps not. Here's the photograph I said I would bring you.

Black Perhaps something at the neck.

Southerndown No. My fiancée is essentially unaffected. Simple. No, unspoiled. Her father . . . I don't want too many sittings. That's why you have these to work from. I shall bring her to meet you next week. (*looking at the portrait*) And this?

Black My next sitter. Due now.

Southerndown Adventurous pose.

Black Do you know him?

Southerndown Know him?

Black Dr Goulderie.

Southerndown Dr Goulderie is my physician.

Black This is his . . . protégé . . . Do you know him?

Southerndown No.

Black There he is now.

Southerndown (*giving him the photograph*) Take this.

Enter Dr Goulderie and Angel.

Goulderie Late. Come. Southerndown!

Southerndown Good day.

Angel You're here.

Southerndown I'm arranging for my fiancée's portrait to be painted.

Angel Is she coming to town at last? Is she going to be allowed into society? Shall we meet her? Or are you going to keep her to yourself?

Black Do you know her?

Angel No one's seen her. Her father . . . (*pointing to Southerndown*) She's changed his life.

Black Are you ready?

Goulderie Yes. Come. Let us begin. Is there heat?

Angel Must I change?

Black If you would.

Angel, laughing, goes behind a screen.

Goulderie (*looking at the picture*) You've worked it up since last we were here. What do you think?

Southerndown The flesh. You'll treat the dress like that?

Goulderie Are you using your box tonight at the opera?

Southerndown What are they giving?

Goulderie The new *Tristan*.

Southerndown I don't think.

Goulderie Go. Wagner is better than injections of chloral hydrate. I'll change your prescription. Where's Boy. Boy.

Southerndown Why do you call him Boy? I called him Beauty.

Angel enters, naked except for a long piece of cloth falling over his shoulder like a towel and a chaplet of coloured flowers in his hair.

Southerndown Let me help.

They help to arrange the pose for the painting.

Goulderie (*at the painting, to the artist*) Look at him and then at this. Less refined, more savage. Like some wretched academician with French brush strokes. Less taste. Less delicacy. I'm a physician. I look at what there is. I don't want anything frankly immodest. I want to show it. If I had wanted something piquant I would have arranged it. Paint him as if he was on a plate. Meat or fruit. Paint what is there. Not this. This is coy, this refinement. This is your refinement. Look, do you see refinement? What do you think you see? Turn, Boy. That's it.

Southerndown Let me help.

Goulderie I must go.

Arthur (*offstage*) Papa.

Southerndown Arthur.

Arthur Papa.

Arthur Southerndown enters carrying a sheaf of lilies.

Dr Goulderie.

Goulderie Hello.

Arthur Where shall I put these?

Southerndown Why are you here?

Arthur I want you to come to my rehearsal, Papa. (*to Angel*) Will you come? Dressed like that, you could be in the show. Here, you have these. (*giving Angel the lilies*)

Angel What is it?

Arthur Something entirely new. Something absolutely new. It's an event. Total theatre. Not a word in it. Tumblers, fire-eaters, a great woman with a snake. Music, singing. It's divine. Dancers on tightropes. Tigers and Chinese dragons. It's a show. A show. An opera for all. (*to Angel*) You'd be divine. Dr Goulderie?

Goulderie No.

Arthur Papa?

Southerndown Not this afternoon, Arthur.

Angel Keep us seats for Friday, Arthur.

Arthur Seats. There aren't any seats. You mill about.

Southerndown Come then, Arthur. Doctor?

Goulderie Oh yes. I'll come with you. (*to Angel*) I'll come for you presently.

Angel No, no. I'll send out. Take a hansom.

Goulderie No, I'll send the carriage. No, I'll come myself.

Angel Don't do that.

Goulderie Yes.

Angel No, darling.

Goulderie Yes, my dear.

Angel No. Please.

Goulderie Well. Well. All right. You'll call a cab?

Angel Of course.

Southerndown, Arthur and Goulderie go.

Black These commissions. This painting with another man's hands. These opinions. Put something up and they know what it should be. Prescriptions and judgements and interference. These intolerable opinions. How can you live with him?

Angel Sh. (*Listens.*) No.

Black Would you like to rest?

Angel No. Go on working. He'll be back. I know he will. I don't know why he left me alone with you.

Black No threat. I'm a servant.

Angel What if he comes back? I'm afraid he'll come back.

Black We're doing nothing. Why are you afraid of him?

Angel Sh. There's someone at the door.

Black It's my servant, sweeping the stairs. Be still. I'm painting your hip . . . There . . . Yes . . . Yes . . .

Angel He'll be back, I know. What shall we do?

Black What do you want to do?

Angel I don't know. I don't know what to do. I don't know how to choose. I'm not used to choice.

Black For you and me, the sky is like lead in a coffin. Or else it breaks up into sunlight and lets in the smell of dead orange blossom which no one has worn.

Angel Why has he left me here? He never leaves me alone. He locks me in.

Black Does he?

Angel But without a key.

Black But he must see his patients. He can't be there all the time.

Angel The servants watch me. I can't leave the house.

Black Why do you put up with it?

Angel Because I have to. Paint me in this. (*He puts on the evening dress.*)

Black No, you mustn't.

Angel Why not? Paint me in this. How do I look in her dress? Paint me in her dress. His fiancée's dress. The doctor would like me in this. At home he likes me to dress up.

Black What do you mean?

Angel Paint me.

Black Tell me. What do you mean?

Angel Slave trousers. Hussar's uniform. Midshipman. You know. Pierrot, faun, drummer boy. He sits and watches or plays the piano. After dinner. Sometimes Southerndown is there. Sometimes one of the others.

Black Why don't you leave?

Angel Why don't you give up painting to commission?

Black I'm tired. This light. I can't go on like this. The colours are dancing in my eyes. Please.

13

Angel We mustn't. He'll ruin you.

Black I don't care.

Angel Don't.

Black Come here.

Angel I mean it. Don't.

Black Yes.

Angel Don't. (*laughing*) Don't. Don't.

Black What do you want? Shall I take my belt to you? Is that what you want?

Angel You'll have to catch me first.

Black Come here then.

Angel You never will.

Black Won't I?

Angel No, you never will. Try it.

Black Come here.

   Chase. He doesn't catch him.

Angel I told you. (*as if talking to a cat*) Come on then. Puss. Puss. Come on.

   Black catches him. Angel disarms him and he falls on to the floor. Angel climbs a ladder.

I'm climbing into the sun.

Black How did I fall?

Angel I can see all the cities in the world.

Black I'm coming after you.

Angel I can reach the sky.

Black I'm holding up the earth.

Angel Take the stars and put them in my hair.

Black Sheet lightning.

Angel Leave me alone.

Black Come down.

Angel No.

    They fall. Angel smashes furniture and china. Mayhem.

I'd like to hunt with a pack of wolves.

Black I've no money to repair all this. You bitch. Look at what you've done. You bitch. I've no one to pour oysters down my throat.

Angel Don't lock the door. He'll be back.

Black I'll belt you.

Angel Will you?

Black I will. He shouldn't have left you.

Angel Will you?

Black No. I love you. Please.

Angel What?

Black Take it off.

Angel It's too cold.

Black Please. Oh please.

Angel You've seen me.

Black That's not seeing you. Please.

Angel Leave me alone.

Black Don't be cruel. Please.

Angel No.

Black Let's go into the other room. Come on. Please.

Angel Why?

Black Because I love you.

Angel What do you want?

Black You know.

Angel In here then.

Black Here!

Angel Don't you want me?

Black You're just being cruel.

Angel You don't want me.

Black I do. I do.

Angel Do you?

Black Yes. Please.

Angel Do you love me, did you say?

Black Take it off, please.

Angel You.

Black What?

Angel Go on.

Black No.

Angel Yes, go on. Go on. Go on.

Black Must I?

Angel Yes, you must.

Black strips to only his shirt.

Unhook me.

In the course of the undressing and kissing Black gets confused.

16

Black I can't do this . . .

Angel is afraid.

Angel Don't kill me.

Punches Black, who falls.

Black Oh. What is it?

Angel Do you want to kill me?

Black No.

Angel Do you? Do you want to kill me?

Black What?

Angel You've never done this before, have you? Poor boy. How old are you?

Black Twenty-eight. And you?

Angel Eighteen.

Black Love me.

Banging on the door.

Goulderie Let me in.

Angel What shall we do? What shall we do? Look at all this.

Black What are you doing?

Goulderie Open this door.

Angel I'll clear up. He'll kill me.

Goulderie breaks the door open.

Goulderie You dogs. Dogs. Dogs. (*spluttering*) Dogs. (*He collapses.*)

Black Dr Goulderie. (*going to him*) Help me then. Help. Leave all this. Send for a doctor.

Angel I think he's dead.

Black Help me.

Angel His nose is bleeding. He must have hit it. He's too heavy. Leave him. Leave him.

Black I'll go for the doctor.

Angel It's too late.

Black We must do something.

Angel Let him go.

Black No. I'll send for the doctor. (*Exits.*)

Angel He'll get up in a minute. Get up – sweetheart. Come, darling. Get up. Get up. Please, my little one. Get up. He's split his nose. His nose is bleeding. Have you had enough of me? Is that it? What shall I do now? Shall I put something on? What do you want? What shall I do? I don't know what to do. I don't know how to do anything. What will I do? Look at his face. Who'll close his eyes?

    Enter Black.

Black The doctor's coming.

Angel Is he? It won't do any good. Close his eyes.

Black What?

Angel We must close his eyes. Will you do it?

Black I can't.

Angel Have you never closed anyone's eyes before this? I'll do it. I'll be dead some day. So will you.

Black Don't say that.

Angel He's staring at me. Look.

Black And at me. I'll do it. (*Closes his eyes.*)

18

Angel I'm rich now.

Black Tell me something.

Angel Yes.

Black Can you love me? Can you love you? Do you believe in love? Tell me. Can you tell the truth? Can you? Tell me.

Angel I'll get dressed. (*Goes behind the screen.*)

Black (*to Goulderie's body*) If I could change places with you. Will you take him back? Is he mine now? Take my youth. I can't have it. I don't know how to live it. I can't cope with happiness. What if I'm happy? What will I do? I can't. I can't. I love him. I do. You can't hear. Please give me the strength to be happy. Give me the strength.

Enter Angel, fully dressed except for his tie.

Angel Do this for me, will you?

TWO

London. A grand drawing room. The portrait from Scene One finished and hanging on the wall. Angel and Black sitting together in the same chair.

Angel Let me go. Let me go. Stop. (*Gets up.*) You see.

Black follows him.

Don't bite me. We're only just out of bed. (*violent*) Leave me alone. Look, these are yesterday's love bites. Why do you want to mark me?

Black You know I've only to hear you walking and I . . .

Angel I'll go barefoot then.

19

Black I'll still hear you. What if you die? What if something happens to you? I wake up each morning and I'm frightened that something's going to happen. That a mad dog will bite you. Today I think there's going to be rioting in the streets. And tomorrow will be something else. I'll get an insect bite and that'll be fatal. I know it will. I can't read the papers. I don't like going out.

Angel (*picking up some letters from a pile on a table*) Have you read this?

Black Yes. It's from my dealer in Paris.

Angel And this?

Black From Moscow. An exhibition.

Angel (*reading*) 'The Duke of . . . is pleased to announce the engagement of his daughter, Lady Adelaide, to Mr Leopold Southerndown.' So at last it's official.

Black I can't understand why it's taken him so long to arrange it. A man with his power and position. We must write to him.

Angel Yes, you do it.

Black I owe everything to you. My success. My happiness. My happiness. All my success is due to you. All this great success. I know it. I would be nothing without you. And you belong to me. You belong to me. I've got to work. Are you angry with me?

Angel No, I'm not angry with you.

Black I think I shall go mad.

Angel I'm sure you will.

Black Don't laugh. I feel I'm screaming.

Angel I know, I can hear you. Is it my fault?

Black No. Nor mine.

Angel Whose fault?

Black It is the fault of your beauty.

Angel But I can't help it. I can't help what I am. I wish I was ugly. I wish I was ugly and a child. So that I could grow up again, look forward. How good it would be to know nothing again.

Black It's your fate, your beauty. It's what can make your kisses so mean.

   Angel kisses Black.

Where did you learn that?

Angel Before I was born.

Black What is it about you? It's not your beauty. It's something else. Have you got a soul, is that it? Is it that you've got a soul?

Angel I want you now.

Black Do you?

Angel Lock the door.

   A bell rings.

Damn it. I've told them to say we're not at home.

Black It might be from my dealer.

Angel It could be from the Queen for all I care.

Black No. I'd better see who it is.

   Exit. Angel alone.

Angel Perhaps it's you you you. Perhaps it will be you you you you.

   Re-enter Black.

Black It's a beggar. Some old-soldier story. I haven't any change. Will you deal with it? I've got to work.

*Goes to his studio. Angel goes to the door and meets
Slavin as he enters.*

Slavin He's not very impressive, is he? He's not what
I anticipated at all. I was expecting something with more
dash. He's a bag of nerves for a start. I thought he was
going to pass out when he saw me. No stomach, eh?

Angel How could you ask him for money?

Slavin It was very easy, my son. That's why I dragged
my poor old bag of bones all this way. I thought you
told me he worked in the morning?

Angel He does. How much do you want?

Slavin Fifty if you've got it. A hundred if you're as flush
as you seem to be. Two of my clients have absented
themselves without prior notice to myself.

Angel I'm so tired.

Slavin That's the two of us. And there's another reason
for my call. I wanted to see this place.

Angel And what do you make of it?

Slavin Reminds me of a time fifty years ago when I had
a bit of luck. Taste differs, of course. That's all. All
Chinese now, I see. I'll be damned if you haven't done
well yourself. Look at the carpets.

Angel What do you want to drink? Tokay?

Slavin Hock and seltzer. Does he drink? The artist.

Angel That would be all I need. This stuff affects different
people in different ways.

Slavin He a violent chap, then?

Angel If he drinks he's out for the count.

Slavin When he drinks you can get him to spill his guts.
Examine his entrails.

22

Angel No. Thank you. So what have you got to tell me?

Slavin That the streets are getting longer and my legs are getting shorter.

Angel I thought you were dead.

Slavin So did I, my dear. But no. When the sun sets we still have to get up in the morning.

Angel How's the mouth organ?

Slavin I'm a bit short of breath. Wheezy. Wheezy like me and the asthma. I'm looking forward to the winter, I am. My asthma might do me the favour of sending me somewhere where there's no return.

Angel They might have forgotten you where you're going.

Slavin That might be so. They might have thought I was earlier on the bill. But tell me about you. It's been so long. Such a long time since I've seen my little boy. My Angel child.

Angel You called me Angel.

Slavin Well, have you ever heard me call you anything else?

Angel I haven't heard it since time was.

Slavin Is there another way of calling you? What do they call you?

Angel It sounds of a time that is gone.

Slavin Don't dance on the streets now?

Angel No.

Slavin Your old accompanist too old and you too old.

Plays the mouth organ. Angel step-dances. Angel laughs and stops. Puts scent on.

Slavin This is what I hoped for you, all this. What's that?

Angel Scent.

Slavin You smell without it.

Angel Not like you.

Slavin What is it?

Angel Heliotrope.

Slavin Heliotrope. And what do you do with yourself all day?

Angel Laze and sleep. Sleep.

Slavin Is that you? (*pointing to the painting*)

Angel It is.

Slavin And is that good, is it? This is how I wanted it to be. I've always believed in your talent, since you were two big eyes and a wide mouth. I've always wanted this for you. And what do you do with yourself? How's your French?

Angel I sleep most of the time.

Slavin It can be very useful, French.

Angel Yes.

Slavin And you cover yourself in Heliotrope and sleep.

Angel So what do you care?

Slavin Why do I care? What do I care? You say that to me. Who'd rather live till the last day and give up any chance of salvation than leave you down here in a tight corner of any sort. What do I care? Have I no compassion, no human frailty, no empathy or sympathy, no human understanding? What do you feel you are?

Angel An animal.

Slavin An animal.

Angel Expensive, well-trained animal.

Slavin A performing animal.

Angel You trained me.

Slavin I could die happy now. I've made my peace with the Lord. I bear no grudges against anyone. Not even against the old dear who washes me and lays me out.

Angel One thing, they can never wash you again. You'd like that.

Slavin You wash, you get dirty again.

Angel It might bring you back, a good wash.

Slavin We're all rotting. We're all dirty flesh.

Angel Not me. I'm luxurious clean. I'm dipped in scent, and my sheets are made of material that nearly matches my skin. I have flesh like fresh fruit: like a peeled apple.

Slavin Rotting fruit. You're good enough to eat. So am I, a feast, good food, I am.

Angel There's not enough on you for worms.

Slavin Don't give me that talk. Your lovers, they won't put you in a preserving jar. You're all right, you, a young man. A nice bit of flesh, but it's not long before you're an old boot and then, who'll know you then? Even the zoo animals will turn their noses up at you. They're particular about what they eat. Bonemeal you'll be.

Angel Don't.

Slavin Have you forgotten who I am? I dragged you out of a hovel and up west with me. Have you forgotten? You were arse-naked, you were. A little naked boy.

Angel How could I forget? You tied me up by the wrists and belted me. I remember that.

25

Slavin It was necessary. It was necessary.

Doorbell rings.

Angel Come on, then. (*Gives him money.*) Will that do you?

Slavin That'll be fine. That'll be fine.

Slavin and Angel go out. Angel returns with Southerndown.

Southerndown I don't understand how you can allow that man into your house.

Angel What's the matter with you? What is it?

Southerndown I must speak to you seriously.

Angel What about, I pray? I saw you yesterday. What's so important today that you couldn't have spoken about it to me yesterday?

Southerndown Does he, Black, know that that fellow was here? If I was him I wouldn't let that creature speak to you.

Angel What is it? Tell me. For pity's sake tell me. What is it?

Southerndown I want you to listen to me carefully.

Angel Why are you so formal? He can't hear. He's in the studio.

Southerndown I should have spoken to you yesterday. I was a damn fool.

Angel Will you listen to me? He can't hear. What is it? What do you want to say? Tell me, what is it? What's the matter? What has happened?

Southerndown Be quiet. You're hysterical.

Angel Then tell me what you want to say to me.

Southerndown This is not easy for me. Not at all easy. Your visits . . .

Angel My what?

Southerndown Your visits to me.

Angel My visits to you?

Southerndown Your visits to me. They must stop. Do you understand me?

Angel No, I don't understand you.

Southerndown It's months now since I first realised that it must finally stop. That it would be better for both of us. For me and for you.

Angel Do you want a drink?

Southerndown No, I don't want a drink. Please listen to me. You must give me this undertaking.

Angel What has happened since yesterday?

Southerndown Things have become clear to me.

Angel Have they?

Southerndown I have asked you twice now. Stop coming to see me.

Angel Are you feverish? Are you hot? Let me feel your forehead.

Southerndown No. I'm fine.

Angel And so am I.

Southerndown If you don't want to hear.

Angel I want to hear. Well?

Southerndown If you don't want to hear what I'm saying, I shall simply tell them not to announce you. They won't let you past the front door. I'll treat you as you should have treated that . . .

Angel There is no need. What have I done?

Southerndown You have done nothing.

Angel Don't play games with me. What have I done that is so wrong? Is it because of the announcement of your engagement yesterday? Do you think I will spoil your chances of finally bringing about this marriage? Is it that?

Southerndown It is that in part.

Angel Is she so pure that I can defile her without knowing her?

Southerndown Don't speak of her.

Angel Then I will be silent.

Southerndown I can't any longer live like this. Live with these . . . differences.

Angel That's not it. How did you get her father to agree?

Southerndown He thinks it's right for her. And I was able to help him recently. My newspapers. He was involved in an unfortunate situation. Not entirely of his making. Stupid of him and typical of –

Angel The mother? You could deal with her only too well.

Southerndown You must see that marriage to such a young woman means that I must regulate my life now.

Angel Fine. Fine. Fine. What do I care about visits. We can meet as you arrange it.

Southerndown There is something I can't make you understand. We are not ever going to meet again. Except in the course of things.

Angel Please don't say that.

Southerndown And how anyhow can you go on treating Black like this?

Angel Don't moralise. You hypocrite.

Southerndown He's a decent enough chap. I've grown quite fond of him. I shall miss his company.

Angel Your marriage will provide you with new friends enough.

Southerndown And I want no unpleasantness with Black.

Angel There's no need for what you call unpleasantness.

Southerndown But he's such a child.

Angel Such a fool.

Southerndown If he weren't a fool he would have found out about you a long time ago.

Angel It might be good for him to smell me as I am.

Southerndown Why are you with him?

Angel Because he's so stupid. And because he thinks he's happy with me. And that pleases me.

Southerndown What if he finds out?

Angel He won't. He doesn't want to. His lack of sophistication is too convenient. He has no idea how ridiculous he is. He thinks his outbursts are a sign of temperament. He's the sexual imagination of an eager young clergyman. He doesn't see beyond his paintbrush and his hysteria. He can't see himself and he certainly can't see me. He's blind. He's blind as a new-born kitten.

Southerndown Does he bore you so much?

Angel What do you think? Sometimes I dream of Dr Goulderie.

Southerndown That old lecher. Because he spoiled you.

Angel At least he wasn't unimaginative.

Southerndown Not with his extensive tastes.

Angel Sometimes I still see him above me. I still see his big face.

Southerndown You miss the discipline, don't you?

Angel I dream often that his burial was a mistake and that he wasn't dead. And that he's still with me. That he never went away. Only he walks softly now in his stockinged feet. He isn't angry with me about the painter. Just sad about it. He seems fearful and timid as if he hadn't got permission to be here again. And he seems part of us. Except he doesn't like it that I've thrown so much money away. But he wants to be here. He comes of his own accord.

Southerndown Well, you must educate the painter into the way of things.

Angel He's in love with me. I can't do that.

Southerndown Fatal to be in love with you. But love doesn't quell the animal in us, you must have seen that. Teach him.

Angel He makes me feel so guilty. I can't bear to look at myself. He doesn't know me at all. He calls me all the names that such a lover knows. Such stupid names. Darling, dearest, puss. You know. But he doesn't know me at all. He thinks I am a woman. He knows nothing about women. He knows nothing about men. He wants to be married, I think. He's afraid of life, of what he might really be. I'm a sort of contraceptive. I am. I count for nothing in his neurasthenic picture of things. He either accuses me of coldness and is violent and then weeps with remorse or is frightened by anything frank and withdraws into an attack of sensibility.

Southerndown Some people would be glad of your power.

Angel Let some people have it then. It's so easy. I have only to put on silk pyjamas and cover myself in scent. He's like a dog and then I have to put up with his grunts. He knows no games, no fun. And then he's very much the man and falls asleep. And of course he's an artist, on top of it all, and thinks he's famous.

Southerndown I assisted a little there.

Angel He wouldn't be capable of understanding. He would think me depraved if he knew. He thinks I lived with Dr Goulderie as a sort of innocent. He thinks I'm a child. And yet I'm glad when he's happy. I am.

Southerndown So it is understood. I want my wife to be happy.

Angel What can you see in her?

Southerndown That should be of no concern to you.

Angel She's as young as I am.

Southerndown She's younger.

Angel Oh, I see. There's that, of course. Am I so old, is that it? You'll die of boredom. She'll kill you with her simplicity. I know. She'll be cheerful. That will bore you. or she'll be quiet and that will bore you even more.

Southerndown She's very biddable.

Angel You'll break her open.

Southerndown Don't be vulgar. And don't try to impede any of this. You have set up an establishment with Eugene Black. There can be nothing between us now.

Angel Oh God. Oh my God.

Southerndown I have done all that I could for you. I made his reputation. You have a great deal of cash which results from my setting you up with Dr Goulderie. You move in society. Now let me be free. I want to live the rest of my life in this new way. Don't compromise what is left of your self-respect by begging me for anything.

Angel You don't want me any more. What shall I do? Do you? Do you? You don't. Well, I shall have to try to deal with this. Shan't I? I shall. I shall have to find a way. I shall. Shan't I?

Southerndown Sh. Sh. Beauty. Boy. Angel, child, darling. What is it?

Angel Since yesterday. Overnight. And it's as if you've never known me.

Southerndown It was going to happen one day.

Angel I won't simply be thrown away. I won't be discarded because of your bid for a place in the world. I don't care for how the world treats me. But not you. Not you. It would be wicked of you. You'll kill me. You will.

Southerndown Do you want more money? Will that do it?

Angel No. I don't want more money. If you belong to anyone in the world you belong to me. I belong to you. You have made me what I am. Everything I have you gave me. You made me. Take me back. I'll do anything. I am your slave.

Southerndown I rescued you. I looked after you. I promoted your career. And now you must let me go.

Angel I smell respectability. You want to be respectable. I don't want to be respectable. I am not respectable. I won't be.

Southerndown If you feel anything for me. If you truly feel any of this gratitude. Then I beg you. Beauty.

Angel Do what you want. Marry her. But don't desert me, please. Please. Don't. I beg you.

Eugene Black enters.

Black What's going on?

Angel He's giving me up. When he's told me a thousand times –

Southerndown Be quiet. Be quiet. Be quiet.

Angel A thousand times he's told me. Like a schoolboy. Stammered how there has never been a love like mine.

Black Leave us alone.

Angel Gladly.

Black Leave us alone. Do as I say. Do as I say.

Angel Tell him. Tell. Him. You asked to be told and you tell him.

Black and Angel go out.

Southerndown This will be hard for him to bear.

Re-enter Black.

Black Is this some sort of foolery?

Southerndown No, it is not.

Black What is it then? Tell me.

Southerndown Shall we sit down? I'm fatigued.

Black What has been going on? Tell me. You must tell me.

Southerndown You must have heard.

Black I heard nothing.

Southerndown Or don't you want to hear anything?

Black I don't know what you mean. Have I displeased him?

Southerndown Oh, pull yourself together man. What does that matter? This is not for children.

Black What does he want of me? What did he mean just now? What's going on?

Southerndown You heard him say what is going on. You heard him say it. Can you hear nothing?

Black Does he want to? Behind my back . . . Others.

Southerndown No. No. That's not it. Let it be now. It's in the past now.

Black What is in the past? What is it? That is in the past?

Southerndown Forget it. You have been happy for months. In heaven, it would seem. Grant him that.

Black What has he done?

Southerndown He told you.

Black You. You. How long?

Southerndown I have known him now for fifteen years.

Black You have been deceiving me.

Southerndown Why can't you grow up? This is not the mirror of middle-class domestic life.

Black I don't understand you.

Southerndown Because you won't listen. I came to put an end to it. I came to tell him it was over. It is over. You must help me to make him understand.

Black You have known him for how long?

Southerndown Since he was seven years old. He used to sell my newspapers outside the Alhambra.

Black He told me he was brought up by relatives.

Southerndown I brought him up.

Black A newspaper boy.

Southerndown Yes.

Black Barefoot?

Southerndown Barefoot, a guttersnipe, a street Arab. I am telling you this so that you will try to understand him. So that you won't imagine it to be all his fault. He has done what he can. His standards are not yours.

Black He said I was the only one.

Southerndown He was lying.

Black On his mother's grave.

Southerndown He never knew his mother. Or her grave. She has no grave.

Black You brought him up?

Southerndown I had him brought up and educated by respectable people. Decent people.

Black And what about Goulderie. Where did he get him?

Southerndown From me.

Black But he didn't touch him, did he? Not really. He didn't touch him.

Southerndown Perhaps he told him that I never touched him either.

Black I saw in him my redemption. I thought God had sent him to me. That he was made for me and I for him.

35

Southerndown The doctor felt much the same thing.

Black Because I was so unhappy.

Southerndown Then accept him for what he is. Or make something of it. Take responsibility for it.

Black Oh God.

Southerndown He has shared all this with you. Grant him that. You have made your life with him. And you have a reputation now. Life is not really over. Don't be such a fool.

Black He told me his life was different. Not that he was . . . That his life wasn't as it was.

Southerndown That's all fooling. Take hold of things. You have money and position. You can't have scruples as well. You love him. Beauty.

Black Who?

Southerndown Him.

Black I call him Darling.

Southerndown The doctor called him Boy. I don't know what his real name is. With such a father. There's little to wonder at.

Black What of his father?

Southerndown He still pursues me.

Black He's still alive?

Southerndown You met him.

Black Where?

Southerndown He was in your house, man.

Black Him? He told me he was lost at sea. That he was lost in a typhoon in the South Seas. Oh God.

Southerndown What is it?

Black Pain.

Southerndown Drink this.

Black My chest. I can't breathe. I can't weep. If I could even cry out.

Southerndown Are you a man? He's worth a million. Who doesn't prostitute himself. You have him. The most beautiful creature in the world.

Black Stop it.

Southerndown This is not a sentimental situation. Take hold of it. Don't lose him. You would be a fool to lose him. Keep hold of him. He is your life.

Black Yes. Yes.

Southerndown He's easy enough to control. You must do it.

Black Yes.

Southerndown Where are you going?

Black To speak to him. To put things right. (*Exits opposite to where Angel has gone out.*)

Southerndown That wasn't easy. He's hard work, that fellow. (*Goes for a drink.*)

    Angel enters from the other side.

Where is he? (*Goes to the door which the artist has used to find it locked.*)

Angel What is it? He's with you.

    Noise off.

What's that terrible noise? Where is he?

Southerndown Open the door.

Angel Where is he? He's doing this . . .

Southerndown Get me an axe. Open the door. Open the door. Get me something. I mustn't be seen here. Get something. Damn you.

Angel He'll open the door. He is making a scene. He'll come out when the storm has subsided.

Southerndown Damn it, get me an axe. Open the door.

Angel I don't know what to do. Open the door. Perhaps we should send for the doctor.

Southerndown Are you a complete fool?

Doorbell.

What's that?

Angel This is your doing, all this. This is your fault. Eugene.

Doorbell.

Southerndown I mustn't be seen here.

Angel It could be his dealer.

Southerndown Be quiet. If we don't answer they'll think that you are not at home.

Angel What's he doing? The noise. Let us in.

Enter Arthur Southerndown.

Arthur Parliament has been dissolved. There are mounted police in . . . What is it?

Southerndown Be quiet.

Arthur What has happened?

Angel Eugene.

Southerndown Get me an axe.

Arthur You look as white as a sheet.

Noise.

God help us. What's happening?

Southerndown Get me something.

Arthur Let me try. (*Puts his shoulder to the door.*)

Southerndown That is of no use.

Arthur What did he find out, Papa?

Southerndown Damned hysterical fool.

Arthur What did he learn?

Southerndown Shut your mouth. What did you come here for?

Arthur The editors are sending for you. They don't know what to do, they need a leading article.

Southerndown Parliament has been dissolved.

Arthur And rioting.

Southerndown Damn this fellow.

Angel enters with an axe.

Angel Here.

Arthur Give it to me.

They smash the door down, it gives way. They go inside. Noise. They come out.

I must sit down. I'm sick.

Angel Blood.

Southerndown I'm ruined.

Angel All blood.

Arthur What did he do?

39

Southerndown His razor.

Angel His head. I can't stay here. Come with me. I can't. I must go and change. (*Exits.*)

Arthur I must remember what this was like. (*Makes a note.*)

Southerndown Well, you can send for the doctor now and the police should be sent for. Where is he?

Arthur He's gone to change.

Southerndown He's destroyed all that I had hoped for in this marriage. In there my prospects are covered in blood.

Arthur You'll find some way of handling things, Father. You always do.

Southerndown You'd like that, wouldn't you? To see this marriage come to nothing.

Arthur Certainly I don't look forward to your second family. Certainly I don't. The thought of you with small children isn't attractive.

Southerndown You've spent a fortune, isn't that what worries you? You've squandered all the money I've ever given you.

Arthur When my mother was alive she made it all right for you with him. Didn't she? She somehow understood how to make it seem all right. And when she died you abandoned him to this. Don't you think you should take him in now?

Southerndown If you're so concerned about him, why don't you take him on? Put him in one of your – what are they? Perhaps I'll fund the pair of you. What shall I do about this?

The sound of gunfire.

Arthur The riots.

Southerndown Parliament dissolved, the government falling. That should take the front page.

Arthur Write an obituary. Write an appreciation of him. The artist. That will do the trick.

Southerndown They will have a field day with this.

Arthur They won't – you'll see that they won't.

Enter Angel.

Angel I can't stay here. Come with me, Arthur, will you?

Door knock.

Southerndown What's that?

Angel It will be the doctor or the police. I sent for them. Isn't that what we should do?

Arthur I must look again. (*Goes into the room where Black is.*)

Southerndown We must tell them of his melancholia.

Angel You've a stain here. Let me clean it for you.

Southerndown It's his blood.

Angel I know. He bled easily. I've seen it before.

Southerndown You monster.

Angel Did you think you could escape me?

Re-enter Arthur.

Arthur As if someone had stuck a pig.

THREE

London. Backstage in a London theatre. A scene change in progress: Buller, the strong-man, has finished his act. Slavin and Hugo, a schoolboy in an Eton collar, are threading their way through all this, watched by the Stage Manager.

Slavin We'd better go this way. Careful now. Watch it.

Hugo Do you think he'll see me? Do you think he'll sign my programme?

Slavin Of course he will. Didn't I say he would?

Stage Manager Out of the way. Come on. Come on. (*to Slavin and Hugo*) Who are you, then? What are you doing here?

Slavin Friends of the artist.

Stage Manager Not backstage during a performance.

Slavin My young friend here . . .

Stage Manager Off you go, then. Go on, there's the pass door. Off you go.

In Angel's dressing room we see Angel closely followed by his Dresser and the Stage Manager, and then Arthur. Angel is dressed in imitation of one of the female stars of the music hall.

You've only got five minutes now. Will you be all right?

Angel I think so.

Stage Manager Are you sure now?

Dresser Come on, love.

Angel (*to the Dresser, going behind a screen to change*) Was it all right?

42

Dresser It was fine. It was fine.

Angel Are you sure?

Arthur I've never seen an audience like it. Never. They're besides themselves, it's a triumph. They love you.

Angel Have you poured me a drink?

Arthur They do. (*Pours champagne and hands it over the screen.*) Here we are.

Dresser Not too much now. We have a performance.

Angel It'll give it fizz. Do you think he's in front? Have you seen him?

Arthur My father?

Angel Yes.

Arthur I don't know. What does it matter?

Angel Are you sure? Do you think he'll come? If he's in, do you think he'll come round?

Arthur If he's in he'll come round. He always has so little time, you know.

Dresser There we are.

Angel She keeping him up to the mark, then? Lady Adelaide, is that it?

Dresser Hold still.

Angel Don't fuss.

Dresser Hold still, then. There we are.

Angel Give me a drink.

The Stage Manager shows Southerndown into the dressing room.

Stage Manager In here. Sir. In here. (*Bars the way to Slavin and Hugo.*) You two. What I say? Off. Shoo.

Slavin The artist is –

Stage Manager Out. (*to Angel*) Five minutes. It's you again next, after the strong-man. How are you doing?

Dresser We're doing fine. Thank you. We know what we're doing.

Angel Who's that? Is it you? It's you. You're in.

Southerndown Quiet. Quiet.

Arthur We were talking about you.

Angel Why have you been so remiss?

Southerndown Remiss? Whose newspapers created all this damned fuss? Eh? They've made this a success, such as it is.

Angel What do you think?

Southerndown There's too much light on the others. Tell them all the light on him. What do you appear as next?

Angel I don't know. Who am I next, Arthur?

Arthur Florrie Forde.

Southerndown Vulgar nonsense.

Angel They seem pleased enough with our efforts. They don't seem to object to what we're doing.

Southerndown Not since my newspapers have been promoting you these past months. (*to Angel*) Have any of your admirers been in to see you? Ha. Ha. I shall go back in front.

Angel Shall we dine afterwards?

Southerndown No.

Southerndown leaves.

Angel I thought he wasn't going to come. He didn't seem to think much of things.

44

Arthur Take no notice of his endless fault-finding.

Angel comes out from behind the screen, wearing a corset and underpinnings. No wig.

Dresser I'll be outside.

Dresser goes out.

Angel He doesn't know how clever you are. He doesn't understand a talent like yours.

Arthur You were unbelievable, you know.

Angel Do you remember when we first met?

Arthur I was back from school. You were in the drawing room. Dressed in blue velvet. My mother was bedridden then. My father had installed you in the house. I was enthralled by you even then. So was my mother. In awe of you. So young. So important to my father. So pampered by my mother.

Angel They had to hide me.

Arthur Yes.

Angel And I remember how you had a toy theatre and how much it engrossed you. I can see you moving the little figures about so intently.

Arthur I was seventeen when she died. And when he sent you away after I told him I wanted you to stay.

Angel Weren't you jealous?

Arthur No, I wasn't. I challenged him to a duel. I thought it was wrong of him. He thinks I have plans to prevent this marriage now.

Angel He can still see me as an obstacle to that. Is she still so unsophisticated, so quiet, so pure? He wants to get rid of me. That's what all this is about. That's why he's put on this show for you. He's hoping some protector will come along. More champagne.

Arthur Haven't you had enough?

Angel Fill it up.

Arthur I hope you don't leave us. I wouldn't like that.

Angel No.

Arthur You were magnificent, you know. You're in your element here.

Angel It's so exciting. They love it so. What would happen if you put life on the stage? Would that frighten them?

Arthur I think it would.

Angel Well, whatever it is, they like it. Even like this. Even with it dressed up like this. What would happen to them if it wasn't?

Arthur I don't know. I've had enough of the art theatre. I wanted something more popular.

Angel But I mean something else.

Arthur How amazing you are. How original you are.

Stage Manager (*coming through the door with the Dresser*) He's on.

Dresser I know he's on.

Stage Manager Why isn't he ready?

Dresser He'll be ready. Where's your dressing gown?

Stage Manager Quick. He'll be off.

Stage Manager, Dresser and Angel go out, taking Angel's new costume and wig with them, leaving Arthur alone. Arthur drinks champagne and makes a note.

Arthur Act One: Doctor Goulderie. Act Two: Eugene Black. Act Three: who will it be?

Commotion off. Buller carries Angel on, puts him down. The Dresser ministers. Slavin and Hugo in the doorway. The Stage Manager enters.

Stage Manager What should we do?

Arthur What's happened?

Stage Manager He passed out. (*Exits.*) Quick, put on the interlude.

Angel I'm all right, get me a drink.

Dresser Come on, let me undo this.

Angel What happened?

Dresser He fainted. Didn't you, dear? Too hot.

Angel Oh. God. She's out front. She's out front. He's brought her with him. How dare he? Did you know? Let me up. Why didn't you tell me? How dare you?

Dresser Let him lie down. Lie down.

Stage Manager He'll go on, won't he?

Dresser He'll go on.

Angel I won't. Not while she's here. I won't.

Stage Manager What'll we do?

Arthur Change the running order.

Dresser We'll get him on.

Stage Manager I'll come back for you.

Arthur I'm coming.

Angel I saw her.

    Enter Southerndown.

Southerndown What is this? What has happened? Out of my way. What is it? What's wrong?

Angel You. How could you do it? Let me up. I'm all right. Let me open and then bring her to see me like this. She's in your box.

Arthur You might have shown some feeling. Isn't this a little brutal?

Southerndown Be quiet. What have you to say that I will listen to? Be quiet. What is this? What is it?

Dresser He passed out. It was them lights, wasn't it, love?

Southerndown Get out.

Dresser What?

Southerndown Get out and you get out. Get out. Get out. Get out.

Stage Manager What shall we do?

Southerndown Get out. Sort it. You sort it. Go.

They all go, leaving Southerndown and Angel.

You've picked up the histrionics easily enough but not the application.

Angel You're making sure, aren't you, that I know my place. Making me appear like this in front of her.

Southerndown You were game enough. And given what you come from, you guttersnipe, you're lucky to be allowed in front of decent people at all.

Angel You can't leave it, can you? It infects everything you feel for me. What I am is where I came from.

Southerndown Nonsense. That's what you trade in. That's what you use. Look at tonight. These gutter hysterics were just an excuse to embarrass a young woman who can hardly keep her seat because of your vulgarity. You're coarse.

Angel I've told you. How often have I told you that I don't care what people think of me. I'm no better than I should be. That's the sum of it. Why should I care about a stupid girl who you bought from a bankrupt aristocrat?

Southerndown You're shoddy stuff, you, aren't you? Eh? This is what you like.

Angel As for coarseness, you'll put her in touch with her coarseness yet. Unlike you, I have never aspired to self-respect.

Southerndown Don't be sentimental. There's gin and a penny gaff about you. Do you think you're any different now from what I found in the streets?

Angel No, thank God. In some ways I'm much the same as I was when I was seven. It's what I've grown into that is so repellent to me.

Southerndown Now. Will you continue with the performance?

Angel Which performance?

Southerndown The one you are paid for.

Angel Which is that? Oh dear. I'm tired.

Southerndown You're not contracted to be tired.

Angel Arthur will understand.

Southerndown Arthur may certainly understand. But I put the money up for this farrago. So this is what you are then, a spoiled performer.

Angel Yes. This is what I've made of all you've given me. No style at all. Have I? Perhaps one of my new-found admirers will take me up. Look. (*Shows him a pack of letters and cards.*)

Southerndown (*picking one up*) Lord Henry Wantage.

Angel Yes. Flowers. Flowers. What he calls his infrequency of flowers.

Southerndown He's not for you.

Angel No. Poor creature. Someone will turn up. One of these. (*dropping the letters*) Perhaps I'll go away. Perhaps I'll go to North Africa with –

Southerndown No. I don't want you to go anywhere.

Angel Why? Why don't you want me to go?

Southerndown Don't look at me. I should go.

Angel Yes. She must be waiting for you. Go then. Go on. I'm not keeping you here.

Southerndown I'll go at the interval. (*He sits.*)

Angel And are you exhausted now? Can't you summon up the energy? With your prodigious energy, can't you find the strength required to marry her? How long an engagement has it been? How many years? You have the energy for everything else. Your schemes. Your newspapers. Your endless capacity for manipulating events. You could give me to Goulderie. You had the energy for that. You could turn the artist into your plaything. You can find the energy to make a duke hand over his daughter against his will. What's stopping you from marrying her, then?

Southerndown Do you flatter yourself that it is you who is stopping me?

Angel Yes. Yes. I do. If you only knew how much pleasure this is giving me. How much I am not regretting this. How I'm enjoying this. You want me to let you go. So that you can put the slum child behind you. But you won't go yourself. You want me to do it. You'll never do it. Try as you will. Get out then. Go then. You see. You won't go. You want me to go. I'm not going. Get out and leave me alone. If you stay you'll make a fool of yourself. You always do.

Southerndown I'm not afraid of you.

Angel I'm not the one you should be afraid of. What do you see in me? You see in me a creature you've imagined, and yet I'm the real thing for you too, aren't I? I'm neither, that's the truth. But you. You swing endlessly between two images of me.

Southerndown Take up with one of these. (*picking up a letter*) I'll be married in a week. And then I'll never have to see you again.

Angel I'll lock all my doors.

Southerndown As there is a God in heaven, I have never hated or regretted anything as I have hated and regretted you.

Angel And all because I was a poor boy.

Southerndown All because you are so wicked.

Angel If you say so. You need to feel that so that you can justify this marriage. Allying that poor creature to someone like you. Oh. Are you going to strike me now? Your wife loved you. But she knew you. This poor girl isn't so wise.

Southerndown Be silent.

Angel Marry her then. Make her perform for you as you have made me perform all this time. Go on. Where's your horsewhip? Do you want me to send for it? Do you?

Southerndown Keep away from me. I must go. I must go home. I can't see her like this. Look at me. Look at me. I can't face them. Any of them. You.

Angel You may be master of all your great enterprises but you'll never be master enough to leave me, will you? You'll never do it.

Southerndown What shall I do? What shall I do?

Angel Here's writing paper. Write this.

Southerndown I can't write.

Angel 'My dear Lady Adelaide.'

Southerndown I call her Adelaide.

Angel 'My dear Lady Adelaide. I write to ask you to release me from our understanding. I cannot in all conscience ask you to link your fate with mine.'

Southerndown Yes. Yes. I can't.

Angel 'I'm unworthy of your love.' Write it. 'The length of our engagement must give some inclination of my ambivalence. I am writing beside the one it is whom I truly love. Forgive me. Leopold Southerndown.'

Southerndown Oh God.

Angel Not oh God. 'My dear.' Post script: 'Do not try to change this.'

FOUR

London. A sumptuous and extravagantly furnished drawing room. Portières, tapestries, several doors, a gallery above. Angel's portrait stands on an easel. Southerndown drinking with Angel and Lord Henry Wantage.

Lord Henry We should be so very honoured if you would come and you might perhaps be amused.

Southerndown What's this?

Lord Henry We intend to re-create for one evening a salon in the French style. In Lord Orchard's rooms in

Half Moon Street. He's undertaking the decoration. We are undertaking to dress accordingly.

Southerndown Can anyone come?

Angel No, not anyone. Not you.

Southerndown I didn't think I would be welcome.

Lord Henry I don't think it would interest you.

Southerndown And why not, pray? No. I don't see myself as Madame du Deffand. (*to Angel*) And you, do you see yourself as a bluestocking, then? I think not. Magnificent flowers. Tuberoses. Tubs of tuberoses at Versailles. Hundreds of them every day.

Lord Henry I think you would make a very convincing bluestocking.

Southerndown Ah. Well.

Lord Henry You'll come?

Angel Perhaps. If you promise to stop sending me so many flowers.

Lord Henry Please. I beg you, don't scold me for sending things that are so humble but more expressive than I.

Angel Twelve chrysanthemums yesterday.

Southerndown Chrysanthemums cost the devil to import. Twelve.

Angel That was yesterday.

Southerndown Worth more than these cigars.

Lord Henry You will come.

Angel What shall I wear?

Lord Henry Perhaps more than you are wearing here. More's the pity.

Angel He doesn't like it.

Lord Henry And the artist, do I know him?

Angel I don't think you would have met him.

Southerndown He cut his throat.

Angel Please.

Southerndown Well he did, didn't he? Dammit.

Angel What's the matter?

Lord Henry I must take my leave. Thank you for receiving me. Your servant.

Southerndown Certainly. *À tout à l'heure.*

  Angel and Lord Henry go out.

(*alone*) This place is unclean. I thought to spend my last days here. And he defiles every corner of it. Arthur too. I know. I know. He too. (*Takes out a pistol and looks behind curtain.*) Where are you? No one here. That doesn't mean that they haven't been there or that they won't be there. Perhaps I should put a bullet through my brain. Family life. Filth and scum. It's all filth.

  Re-enter Angel.

Angel Do you have to go out?

Southerndown What did that fool really want?

Angel You heard what he wanted. Let's take the carriage and drive through the park. (*arms round his neck*)

Southerndown Today I'm going to the Stock Exchange, as I usually do, as you know I do. Today I have to watch everything. Do you want me to lose what little I have in the markets? (*Southerndown injects himself with morphine.*)

Angel You said you would stop that.

Southerndown Did I? I suppose I did. Well, you don't normally see this, do you?

Angel Why are you so sad?

Southerndown I wish I could laugh.

Angel Laugh, try it.

Southerndown I love your profile more than Lord Sheffield does his string of racehorses.

Angel It would be better to die, I think, than to be merely miserable.

Southerndown That sounds fine enough.

Angel I think it would be easy to die.

Southerndown Here we are then. You and I.

Angel Yes, me and you, as I chose it.

Southerndown It was a daring choice. I should laugh.

Angel Try it.

Southerndown I shall.

They go off. Lord Henry enters from another door. Comes in hesitantly. On hearing voices, hides.

Lord Henry I thought he might be alone. Someone's coming. I'll hide.

Enter Buller, Slavin and Hugo. Buller carrying Hugo.

Slavin Come on, boys. There we are. It's good to be home. Who polished those stairs, eh? You could break your neck easy. This place is a death trap. Come on then, don't worry, we'll be all right. Now. What'll it be? Here we are. (*Pours drinks.*) What do you want? It's all here. Will he have one? He'll have one.

Buller He's not big enough, are you? He's not big enough to walk yet, let alone drink.

Hugo You put me down. I'll show who's big enough when the time comes.

Buller He's no more than eight stone.

Hugo Put me down. I shall be expelled from school for this.

Buller We'll give you schooling all right. You'll get your schooling all right from me and this gentleman. Eh?

Slavin Yes, many's the man's won his medals with the person you're going to meet here.

Hugo What shall I say to him?

Slavin Don't you worry. You won't have to say anything. He'll see to that.

Hugo I wrote a poem yesterday.

Buller A poem. What you write a poem for?

Slavin What he write?

Buller A poem.

Slavin Oh, a poem. Very good. (*to Buller*) He promised to see me all right if I arranged a meeting and then left them alone.

Buller He got the cash then?

Slavin His father does. He's an appeal court judge. A cigar? No. Yes. I thought you would.

Hugo Who lives here anyway?

Slavin We do.

Buller Every week we come here when the master's at the Stock Exchange.

Hugo What shall I do with it? Shall I read it?

Buller What's he on about now?

Slavin His poem. Poets are like that. He's going in for elaborate foreplay. Look at his eyes. Look at his eyes.

Buller With eyes like that there's no chance for us. Look at them.

Slavin No chance at all. Have we? We haven't. You're drunk.

Buller Am I?

Slavin You're pickled.

Enter Angel.

Angel What are you up to, eh? What you doing here? Eh?

Buller (*to Slavin*) Your health, you old thief.

Slavin (*to Buller*) Your health, you great ponce.

Angel I'm expecting someone. (*to Hugo*) What are you doing with these two, eh? Don't be shy, eh? Those are not fit companions for you. What are you doing now? With this boy?

Slavin He's not a boy. He's a poet.

Angel Enough. You.

Buller (*to Angel*) Here. Can you lend me fifty pounds? My old woman. My wife, see.

Angel Are you married?

Buller 'Course I'm married. Only she's poorly, see. Bad health. Consumption. I need the cash for her. Ten quid then. Come on, eh? Come. (*Puts his arms round Angel.*) Let's get drunk, eh? Let's get out of here. Let's leave them two. Come on, you want to. You know you do.

Angel Do I?

Buller No. All right. Well then, let's meet then. Out of here. One night. No good here. What do you say?

Angel I don't know.

Buller Don't you? I need the money. Honest I do. Try these. (*Takes his shirt off. Shows his muscles.*)

Angel We all know how big you are.

Buller Try 'em.

Angel Yes.

Buller Come on then. Come on. I don't understand you. I don't. I don't know what you want.

Angel If only your ears were different.

Slavin Who you expecting then? You expecting Lord Henry?

Angel Good Lord, no. God forbid.

Lord Henry hears this.

Buller Who's he then?

Slavin He's going to carry him off.

Angel Indeed he isn't.

Slavin We all want to do that.

Buller Do you want to do that? Take him away from all this?

Slavin We all do.

Buller You don't. I thought he was your boy.

Slavin No.

Buller So who's his father then? I thought you were.

Slavin No. He ain't never had a father. Have you?

Angel What have I never had?

Slavin A father.

58

Angel No. I'm a physical impossibility. Come on, out you go, he'll be back.

Buller Where we going?

Angel Off you go.

Slavin He's at the 'change.

Angel You never know.

Slavin Gor blimey. In my own home.

Buller I'll sort him out.

Angel Will you? We'll see how big you are if he comes in here. If only your ears were different.

Enter Frederick, a footman.

Frederick Mr Southerndown.

Slavin It's him. Blimey, the bastard's back. That's not part of my plan, not at all. That's not the arrangement by any means. He's become very unreliable. Come on. Give me the key.

Angel What for?

Slavin To lock myself in upstairs.

Angel Shall I see you later?

Hugo goes under the table. Buller hides at the opposite side to Lord Henry. Slavin goes upstairs.

Slavin Give us the bottle.

Enter Arthur Southerndown.

Arthur I've come from the theatre. We're experimenting with electric light. Who in heaven's name is that?

Slavin hasn't yet quite got off.

Angel A friend of your father's.

Arthur I haven't seen him before in my life.

Angel They were in the army together. He's fallen on hard times.

Arthur He's not here is he, my father?

Angel They had a drink and then your father went into the city. I've ordered luncheon.

Arthur No lunch for me.

Angel I've ordered. It's nothing much.

Arthur I can't eat.

Angel You try something. What is it?

Frederick enters with a tray, a bottle of champagne and oysters. Lays the table.

Arthur What's the matter with him? Are you all right?

Angel Let him be, Arthur.

Arthur You seem out of sorts.

Frederick Yes, sir.

He goes. Arthur goes to Angel.

Angel What's this, Arthur?

Arthur You promised.

Angel What did I promise?

Arthur You as good as promised.

Southerndown enters in the gallery.

Southerndown I knew it. My own son.

Angel What have I promised?

Arthur You look flushed.

Angel Do I? When I looked in the mirror a little while ago I wished I was a man.

Arthur Indeed.

Angel And then I wished I was a woman. Then I could marry myself. Be inside myself.

Arthur You envy the pleasure others have in you perhaps, is that it?

Angel Is it? Why are you like this?

Arthur You proposed this assignation as something special. Or you hinted at something special.

Angel Did I? Why are you so, well, overheated?

Arthur You know why. When I'm out riding in the park. When I'm lying in my room. When I'm working. You are in my head. Not in my head, I can feel you. I can smell you. Coming here, rattling in the cab. Everywhere. The thought of you always. The sense of you on my hands, in my nostrils. I smell you. I shall spill over. I can see how a man could be a sex murderer.

Angel I should like to be murdered in that way. Perhaps I would be inside myself then.

Arthur I can sense you all the time.

Frederick re-enters. Clears. Serves another course.

What is the matter with you?

Angel Leave him alone, Arthur.

Arthur Have you got a fever, old man?

Frederick I'm not used to working in the house, that's all. I'm one of the grooms, only in here today.

Southerndown Is he another of them, the groom? Is that it?

Angel Come along, eat something.

Arthur What's this? (*indicating the table*)

Angel Nothing, it's me. My foot.

Arthur Why have you asked me here? Why? You must know how I feel. Why here?

Angel Because I admire you. I respect you. Because I wanted to see you. Is that wrong of me? You have always respected me. You've always stood up for me, Arthur. Always. Even against your father.

Arthur Don't let's talk about all that. That's my unfortunate character.

Angel Don't, you are good, Arthur.

Arthur And I don't want to be good. I'm not good. I'm not just his son. I'm not your brother.

Angel Aren't you? I always think you are my brother. Aren't I allowed that? That's why I've been able to talk to you. Who else can I talk to?

Arthur I'm one of those wicked people who are cursed with an impulse for good.

Angel Arthur.

Arthur Yes. Do you know what it is to be like that and to experience the disintegration of oneself? I'm disintegrating. Sometimes I feel I am. (*He looks under the table.*)

Angel What is it?

Arthur I don't know. I know that the more I try to control myself the more I'm going to pieces. You've always been something to be in awe of. A kind of saint, in spite of your talent for seeming the contrary.

Angel What is it like, this feeling of not being there, then?

Arthur Please don't make me speak of it. Please. I don't want to be the subject of interest over a glass of champagne. The experience to which I allude has been one of the joys of life, I assure you. A complete pleasure.

Angel I've hurt you. I didn't mean to. I won't allude to it again. Here's my hand.

Arthur (*kisses his hand*) Please.

Buller pokes his head out. Angel sees him and signals him back. He goes back. Hugo pokes his head out from beneath the table. Angel kicks him.

Southerndown (*alone*) Another of them.

Arthur I feel like someone who has died and is rubbing the sleep out of his eyes as he wakes up in heaven. Your eyes are glittering like water in a well after a stone has been thrown in. Your hand. There's oil here. Let me lick it. (*Licks his hand.*) You are above me. Like the sun shining over an abyss. You. Let me kiss your feet.

Kneels. Angel stands.

Destroy me, then. Finish me. If you want to.

Angel You love me. (*to Frederick*) Bring coffee. Cognac.

Arthur Where shall we drink it?

Angel Let's go to my room.

Buller pokes his head out. Tries to signal to Southerndown to shoot Arthur. But Southerndown points gun at Buller. Angel sees Southerndown.

Your father.

Southerndown (*points the gun at Arthur*) Arthur. (*He comes down.*)

Arthur Papa.

Southerndown Parliament has been dissolved.

Arthur Papa.

63

Angel What should I do?

Southerndown Go to the office. Tell them I sent you. Tell them I will be there soon. (*Pointing revolver at him, takes him out of the door.*)

Buller makes a dash for it.

Angel You can't go that way.

Buller Let me through.

Hugo looks out. Lord Henry crosses the room to another hiding place.

Angel You'll run straight into him.

Buller He'll put a bullet through me.

Angel Quick, he's coming.

Buller Christ. (*He tries to get under the table.*)

Hugo No room. Sorry.

Buller All I wanted was fifty quid.

Buller hides where Lord Henry was. Re-enter Southerndown. He goes to where he thinks Buller is.

Southerndown Where is he?

Angel He's gone.

Southerndown Where's he gone?

Angel He's an acrobat.

Southerndown Is he, be damned. I can't have been expected to know that. Now you. Now you. Animal. You animal. You want to kill me with your endless depravity.

Angel You taught me how to do it.

Southerndown This is my fate, then, is it? Either to drown in your sewage or to be hanged for the pleasure of murdering you?

Angel Kill me then, if you must do it.

Southerndown I've left everything to you and all I asked was the courtesy one could expect from a weekend guest. Your credit has run out. You backstreet whore.

Angel My security is good for a few years yet.

Southerndown You're like a fatal disease I've contracted. And I've been hoping all this time for a cure. And I've found it. Here it is. But it's for you to take.

Handing him the revolver. Angel plays with it.

Angel I can't fire it.

Southerndown Can't you indeed? Pray let me instruct you. (*Takes the revolver back.*) How beautiful you still are to me. From beyond the sunset. I would like to curl up against you, feel your body cupped into mine for the last time and then kill you.

Angel Put the revolver down. Put it down. Forgive me.

Southerndown It's the morphine. All this. It must be. I forgave you long ago. I must kill you or see my son drown in his own blood when I have killed him.

Angel You love me too much to do it.

Southerndown Do I? I suppose I do. Yet I must kill you.

Angel Or punish me then. Or beat me then. Belt me till I bleed. I won't scream or cry out. I'll bite my handkerchief. (*Takes out his handkerchief and bites on it.*) Or let's go to the opera. Don't kill me. Let me go. Please don't kill me. Don't. I want to piss.

Southerndown It's hardly worth it now. Here, I'll show you how to use it. Do you see? (*Shows him the workings of the revolver.*) Do you see?

Angel No.

Angel shoots at the ceiling. Buller runs out from his hiding place.

Southerndown Who's that?

Angel A bird flying from its nest.

Southerndown Who else is here? (*He finds Lord Henry.*) Where did you come from? Down the chimney?

Lord Henry Don't let him kill me.

Southerndown Have you come to lunch?

Lord Henry No. No.

Southerndown Yes. Yes. Stay to lunch. All of you stay to lunch. Where's the groom? Let him come to lunch. (*He pushes Lord Henry out of the door.*)

Angel Come, let's go out. Let's go for a drive.

Southerndown Are you going to shoot me then? It would be the happiest moment of my life. Do it.

Angel Well, let's agree to part, then. Let's do that.

Southerndown We part? How can you be so utterly foolish. How could we part? Part so that I could see someone else find his pleasure where I once fell into hell. . . Facing suicide with you still in my sight. We are part of one another, you and I. I can see your next victim lying on your bed. He's longing for you. Isn't he? Give me the revolver.

Angel No.

Southerndown Kiss me. Kiss me. (*turning Angel's hand on himself*) Come on, use it. You can use it. You can handle it. Squeeze it softly. Do it. Do it. Feel it. Can you feel it? Feel it.

Angel I must piss.

Southerndown Do it.

Angel Shall I? Shall I? Shall I do it? Shall I? I'll do it for you, shall I? No. (*Pushes Southerndown away.*)

Southerndown injects himself with morphine.

If men have killed themselves because of me, does that mean I am then valueless? You have always known from the beginning what you were doing when I didn't know, or I have known it for some of the time – what I was doing. But you always. You took my childhood and my youth as if they were yours to do with. And I have taken your old age. Was it a fair exchange? I have never wanted to be taken for anything but what I am. You want me to put a bullet in my heart. But I won't. I may not be seven any more. Nor sixteen. But I'm not yet twenty. I won't do it. I can't do it.

Southerndown On your knees then, murderer. You murderer. Ask God to give you the strength.

During the struggle Hugo jumps up from under the table.

Angel No. No. Help. Help.

Southerndown turns as Hugo runs out, presenting his back to Angel who shoots him five times. Southerndown falls into Hugo's arms.

Southerndown (*as he falls to the floor*) And you're another of them, are you?

Angel Dear God.

Southerndown Out of my sight. Arthur.

Angel The only man I have ever loved.

Southerndown Water.

Angel Get him some water.

67

Arthur enters.

Arthur Father. Father.

Angel I shot him. Give him this.

Hugo It wasn't his fault. It wasn't.

Southerndown (*to Arthur*) He's yours now. Take him.

Arthur Come, let's get you to bed.

Southerndown No, leave me. I'm thirsty.

Angel gives him champagne.

Champagne. You don't change, I see. Thank you. (*to Arthur*) You'll be the next.

Lord Henry comes in.

There's another of them. Only he's a fool. Fool.

Angel He's dead.

Arthur Don't move from this room.

Lord Henry I thought it was you who had been shot.

Arthur Get the police.

Angel Don't, Arthur, please.

Arthur Get them.

Angel Please, Arthur. I'll do what you want. Whatever you want. Don't do this, please. I beg of you. Look at me, Arthur. Look at me. Arthur. I beg you. I beg you. Arthur.

Doorbell.

Arthur That will be the police.

Hugo This means I'll be expelled.

FIVE

London. The drawing room as in Scene Four, but almost bare. Angel's picture on the floor turned to the wall. Gunshot.

Tableau: the moment of Angel's shooting of Southerndown. Everyone involved frozen as they were then. Slavin walks through them and speaks to the audience.

Slavin You'll remember where we were. Well now then. There was Angel's arrest then.

Tableau: Angel being handcuffed by the police.

And of course the boy.

Tableau: Hugo arrested in flight.

And after the usual charges and the magistrate and the putting up of the bail and the waiting and the newspapers. Leopold Southerndown's newspapers. The trial.

Tableau: Angel in the dock.

And Arthur's plea for clemency.

Tableau: Arthur in an attitude of appeal.

And defending his father's killer. The charges of murder were dropped and charges of manslaughter replaced them. And Angel was sentenced.

Tableau: Angel under sentence.

For ten years.

Tableau: Angel being taken down to the cells.

And then Lord Henry.

Tableau: Lord Henry tries to pull Angel away from his captors.

Lord Henry.

Tableau: Lord Henry alone and dejected.

Lord Henry, who had financed the whole defence. Strewth. Paid for the whole lot, he did. Paid for the lawyers, the solicitors, the barristers. Paid for it all. And that was not all he did. That was not all.

Tableau: Lord Henry seated with a shawl around him. Near Arthur, pensive. Buller dressed as a servant.

You'll see.

Tableau relaxes into action.

Buller What's keeping the old man then, eh? Why's he keeping us hanging about, then? We got to get off.

Lord Henry Please. Please.

Buller What beats me is how you think he can possibly have been changed for the better by it all.

Lord Henry He is more refined and beautiful now than I have ever seen him before.

Buller Well, I don't know that I can take your word for it as far as looks go, if cholera has done for him what it's done for you. Look what it's done for you and look at me. All this has put me right out of condition.

Lord Henry What puts some people in the grave has restored him like a resurrection.

Buller Well, that's all fine and dandy. But I've had enough of this. I'm not going with him tonight. I've decided he and the old man'll have to manage without me.

Lord Henry Are you going to let him travel alone? I thought Mr Southerndown had arranged things with you. Is there something wrong with the arrangement? Is it financial? Can I change your mind?

Buller The old man'll be with him. He'll be all right. It's sorted.

Lord Henry Mr Southerndown. The travel arrangements have been altered.

Arthur What's that? I beg your pardon. I haven't been listening. (*Makes a note.*) I've been working at an idea in which someone has been sentenced to penal servitude and wondering if it was a suitable subject for a play nowadays. What do you think?

Lord Henry The travel arrangements are altered. They're to go without protection.

Arthur Lord Henry. Forgive me. I don't wish to appear discouraging but I'm not at all certain that your plans for his escape are, well, feasible, anyway. Although I can't find words to express my admiration for all that you have done. Your selflessness. The sacrifices you have made. Indeed your extraordinary enterprise. I have no idea, Lord Henry, and I mean no offence. Well, I have no idea, well to be blunt, how wealthy you are. But the expenses you must have incurred in the case of this enterprise must have, how shall I put it, disorganised your finances. May I offer you the loan of, well, would ten thousand pounds be useful at all? I can make it available to you in cash. It would be no problem.

Lord Henry He has been so brave. You know. All the times we were in the hospital ward together. And so kind to me. So full of tender words. And full of promises for the future.

Buller For one thing, I've got to wait here until the costumes are ready for the new act. I'll get another boat all right. He'll be all right with the old man. I wouldn't have got involved in this if he hadn't done me a few favours and I didn't fancy him before and you hadn't taken me on as his protector. We'll get an act together in

Paris. They'll appreciate me in Paris. When I've got fit again. They're more broad-minded abroad anyway. We'll work something up together – you'll see. Here they don't know talent when they see it. I got done for indecency not two years ago. Give me a fifty-bob fine.

Arthur I find it much the same with my work. When I gave up first the art theatre and then the popular theatre after my father's death, I felt myself moved towards a more serious theatre. So I wrote a play about what happened. A play dealing with the death of a man like my father and the person who had done it and how it had come about, and so forth. But they wouldn't license it. It was thought to be improper. Some people read it in Gordon Square.

Lord Henry Sh. Here he is.

Slavin (*off*) Yes, here I am. Here I am.

Enter Slavin.

Slavin I've been all over the place this morning. Selling this and that. Bits and pieces. Sorting things out. Tidying up loose ends. Disposing of my assets. Fixing the papers, getting the passports sorted.

Buller I've got a good hotel for you in Paris. The people who run it come from Bermondsey.

Lord Henry Help me up. I beg you.

Buller You'll be safe from the police here. Safe as houses.

Slavin Where will you be, then?

Lord Henry He wants you to go with him alone. Just the two of you. Without his protection.

Slavin What, you scared, eh? Scared of the cholera and scared of the law. Eh? What's put the wind up you?

Buller Nothing has. I ain't scared. I've got to get the props for my new act sorted out, haven't I? I told 'em. I'll have to come on later.

Arthur Please take this money, Lord Henry. Please do. There's two thousand pounds here I cashed especially.

Lord Henry That's kind of you. But no, I thank you.

Arthur Please. I beg you. Take it.

Lord Henry Please let us go now.

Slavin Patience, my dear Lord Henry. It's no distance to the hospital. You'll be there in no time. I'll be back, with him in tow in five minutes, just you see.

Arthur You bringing him here?

Slavin I am certainly bringing him here. Are you scared too? What's the matter with you all?

Arthur No. I'm not frightened of anything. A sort of apprehension, I suppose.

Slavin Come, Lord Henry. Off we go. Off we go.

Lord Henry and Slavin go out. Arthur locks the door.

Buller Why did you want to give money to that madman? That hopeless excuse for a man.

Arthur What, pray, has that to do with you?

Buller Because of the pittance you pay me. Even though I had to bribe every nurse in the isolation hospital and the young doctors and the porters. And then you offer him all that cash. I had to spend three months in that hospital getting information. Squaring things. Sorting things out. Now I'm too fat for work and too caught up in all this for the authorities but to watch me – and so I became your servant. And I'm to go to Paris, ain't I, to look after him? Work up the act. What more can I do for you all, eh? And what for?

Arthur Lord Henry has paid you handsomely for your services and covered every expense which you have incurred. And according to my estimate, apart from what you get from me, he also provides you with a monthly allowance of ten pounds. So I really do find it hard to believe that you have done anything out of love and concern for the man we're waiting for so anxiously. I do, however, think it probable that you have exploited Lord Henry shamelessly and taken part in this enterprise only for your own advancement. You'd have ended up in the gutter else, I dare say. Drunk and penniless.

Buller And what about you, eh? Then what about you? What would you be if you hadn't sold your father's fish-and-chip papers, from what I heard, for a million pounds. A million pounds. What would you do if you had to do a day's work, eh? What would you do? All you've done while he's been inside is write something no decent person wants to see, about a bum boy and morphine addict. Which no one'll put on because what the public wants is more in my line of things, ain't it?

Door knock.

Who's that?

Arthur It's him. I haven't seen him for a year.

Buller No, it can't be him. Well open the door then, for Christ's sake. What's the matter with you?

Arthur You hide yourself while I see who it is.

Buller hides. Arthur goes to the door. Hugo comes in.

And who are you, may I ask? You. It's you. What do you want? Why are you here? What have you come here for?

Hugo I escaped from the reformatory this morning. I've travelled all this way. I've come straight here.

Arthur What do you want here?

Hugo Please. I've come to help. I want to help him. I've worked up a plan to help him to escape.

Arthur What are you talking about? What kind of plan? What do you want?

Hugo Please help me. Can anyone hear us? Please, I beg you. You can't be so indifferent to his plight. It was your evidence that saved him from the gallows.

Arthur I know who you are now. You said my father tried to make him kill himself.

Hugo He did. He did. But no one would believe me.

Buller comes out with a tray of coffee.

Buller Would the young gentleman take his coffee in the drawing room or on the terrace?

Hugo What's that fellow doing here? He came out of the same door then. That's the same door.

Arthur I've taken him into my service. He's quite useful. He can throw people out.

Hugo I'm a fool to be here. I'm a fool.

Buller Yes, we know each other, this young gentleman and me. Don't we, eh? What you doing here? Don't you know he's dead, your sweetheart? He's dead.

Hugo Did they hang him after all then, did they? It's not true. How do you know? How do you know? You don't know.

Buller Read this then. Where is it? Read this then. (*Shows him a newspaper.*) 'Mr Leopold Southerndown's killer struck down with cholera.'

Hugo 'The killer of Mr Leopold Southerndown has contracted cholera in prison.' It doesn't say he's dead.

75

Buller Cholera. He's dead all right. Buried three weeks ago in the cemetery not a little way from here. By the rubbish dump. Little crosses with no name. You'll recognise it, it's got no grass growing. Go and pay your respects, then go back to the schoolroom, or I'll hand you over to the law. I'll follow you.

Hugo It's true. Is he dead, then?

Arthur Yes. I thank God, he's dead. Please leave us now. I'm unwell.

Hugo What point is there now? I have no future now. What's the point of anything. I wanted to save him. I would have, too. Made him happy. Well, I'll go to the devil another way.

Buller No, get out. Go on. Off you go.

Arthur Yes. If you would go.

Hugo I've been a fool.

Buller Off you go.

Hugo exits.

I'm surprised you didn't offer him cash payment as well.

Arthur Spare me your humour. That boy has more honour in him than you in your great body.

Buller What's that?

Arthur Is that him? Here he is. Here he is.

Angel enters dressed in Lord Henry's clothes and wearing his shawl. He is walking with difficulty, supported by Slavin.

Slavin Gee up. Come up, my little Angel. We've got to cross the Channel tonight.

Buller Hell and damnation. Look at him. Look at him.

Angel Slower please. I can't go as fast as you.

Buller Where did you get the nerve to break out looking like that? Like a starved wolf, you look.

Slavin Shut your mouth, you.

Buller I'm not having anything to do with this. How's he going to make it to Paris? Look at him. Look at him. What do you expect me to do with him? I'm going to turn you in, the lot of you.

Arthur I must ask you to be quiet. I must ask you to show some understanding. Angel.

Buller Don't talk to me about understanding. Look what I've done for him. Ruined my career. Look at me. Look how fat I am. Fit for a clown. I'm going to turn you in. The lot of you. (*He goes.*)

Slavin He won't go to the law. I know him. He wouldn't risk it. He'll be back. Where else he got to go?

Arthur Here's some coffee. Shall I pour some for you?

Slavin Hurry up then. I've still got to book our berths.

Arthur Here we are. (*dispensing coffee*)

Slavin (*after drinking his coffee*) Right. I'll be off then. I'm scuttling all over the place. Got to sort out some business. I'll get the tickets and be back for you. You all right?

Angel I'm all right.

Slavin Mr Southerndown, your most humble. Enjoy yourselves, my children. Drink your coffee. (*Sings.*)

Oh I'd like to go again
To Paris on the Seine,
'Cause Paris is a proper pantomime.
And if they'd only take the 'Ackney Road
And plant it over there
I'd like to live in Paris all the time.

Honi soi. (*Leaves.*)

Angel Free. Oh God. Am I?

Arthur Would you like a drink? A brandy with your coffee?

Angel I can't believe how big this room is. I haven't been in a room for two years. Look at the curtains. Where's my picture?

Arthur Are you still so vain?

Angel Yes. It's frightening when you haven't seen yourself for months. I found an old piece of tin in prison and cleaned it up as best as I could. It wasn't very flattering. But it was reassuring to see that I was still there.

Arthur Here it is. (*showing the picture*) It was turned to the wall. Lord Henry wanted it in his house, but it seemed more prudent to keep it here.

Angel Haven't you looked at it at all while I've been away? And now Lord Henry is taking my place in the prison hospital.

Arthur I don't understand how it happened. How was it all arranged?

Angel Oh he arranged it all very carefully.

Arthur How can you be so cold about it?

Angel I don't know. I admire him and his courage. I'll tell you. There was an outbreak of cholera in Liverpool this summer and Lord Henry saw this as the way to get me out. He worked as an auxiliary nurse. Through his university settlement, you know. And good works among the poor. They could hardly turn him down. Well, nothing daunted, Lord Henry took infected clothing from a man who had died. He was given the things to put in the furnace. But instead he put them on. And then he travelled back to visit me, wearing them under his

78

street clothes, and we exchanged some of the dead man's clothing. He was already coming down with cholera.

Arthur And you came down with it too?

Angel And we both found ourselves in the isolation hospital. There was no question of my staying in the prison for fear of infecting others. So we were together in the same ward. He was discharged yesterday. And today he came back on the pretence of having lost his wristwatch and we exchanged clothes. And I walked out. It was easy. And now he is serving the sentence for having murdered your father.

Arthur You still bear comparison to your portrait.

Angel Older. Thinner.

Arthur You look better than you did when you came in.

Angel Come here. Aren't you going to kiss me?

Arthur Shall I?

Angel Are you afraid?

Arthur Your eyes are glittering. Glittering.

Angel Come here.

Arthur Your mouth is thinner.

Angel Am I repulsive, then?

Arthur Oh, now I shall write a poem about your eyes and your mouth.

Angel These awful clothes.

Arthur They make you look more striking.

Angel Look at these terrible shoes.

Arthur Please. Let us be grateful for what we've got.

Angel I can't now. I will. What shall I do about Lord Henry? At my feet begging me to punish him. What shall I do about him?

Arthur Please.

Angel No. Not yet. I shot your father in this room, remember.

Arthur I know but that doesn't stop me loving you. Kiss me. Kiss me.

Angel Hold your head back. (*He kisses him.*)

Arthur You still know how to control me. You're the most dangerous man who ever brought anyone to ruin. But your eyes say something else.

Angel Come with me tonight to Paris. We can be together there. I missed you. If you come with me we'll be together.

Arthur I can feel you under all this. Let me. See you. Please. These awful clothes. Please. I can feel you. The shape of you. Let me feel you.

Angel sags. Arthur supports him.

Please let me feel you. I'm making love to a sick man. I can feel how frail you are.

Angel Will you come with me?

Arthur This is driving me mad. What am I doing to you?

Angel Will you?

Arthur But Buller and the old man are going with you.

Angel We'll get another berth. We shouldn't. This is where your father bled to death.

Arthur Sh. Sh.

SIX

*Paris. A white drawing room. Eighteenth-century
furniture. Angel's portrait set in a sumptuous frame.
Doors at the back through which we can see a gaming
table and Turkish furniture and rugs. Angel, Lord Henry,
Arthur, the Marchese di Casti Piani, Baron St Eglise, Weil,
Phillipeau, August, Baptiste, Hippolyte, surrounding
Buller, who is making a toast.*

Buller Gentlemen, gentlemen. Thank you. Please charge
your glasses. And join me in wishing our host good
wishes on his birthday. Damn it.

   They all toast Angel.

Arthur (*to Buller*) Well done. Well done, old man.

Buller I'm sweating like a pig

Baptiste (*to Buller*) They tell me that you're the
strongest man in the world.

Buller And so I am. So I am. My strength is at your
disposal.

Hippolyte I prefer marksmen myself. To strong-men.
There is a man at the casino who shoots from the hip.

Marchese (*to St Eglise*) Tell me, old man. Where did you
find him? How old is he? He's enchanting.

St Eglise Isn't he? This is his first time out.

August Are you talking about me?

Marchese I was hoping that you were having a good
time.

August I am. Thank you.

Baptiste Champagne. (*Takes August away.*)

81

Phillipeau Pretty mouth.

Marchese Pretty figure.

St Eglise Now. Now. Let us remember ourselves, shall we? He's too young for you.

Marchese They're never too young for me, my dear St Eglise. How much?

St Eglise He's not for sale.

Marchese Uncut diamonds.

St Eglise You're not to be trusted.

Hippolyte Are we going to play?

Baptiste Of course. Let's go in.

Hippolyte Are we playing, Lord Henry?

Lord Henry May I join you presently?

Marchese Can I play with you? Shall we split the stake? You always have such a lucky hand.

Baptiste We'll go in to hell together.

They link arms, Marchese, Baptiste and Hippolyte, and go into the gaming room.

St Eglise (*to Weil*) How are the Jungfrau shares holding up, Weil?

Weil (*to Phillipeau*) He's talking of the new cable railway in the Alps. It's amazing. That's why they're doing so well. Well, I still have four hundred but I'm keeping them for my own use. There's a fortune to be made in them.

Phillipeau I have some. A few. I'd like to accumulate more. Do you think . . .

Weil We'll see what we can do.

St Eglise My astrologer told me to buy. I've put everything into them. If they fail it will be your fault. Your fault, Weil.

Weil They'll be fine. They'll be fine.

Arthur Yes. They're sound. Sound. I paid through the nose for mine. I put everything I had left into them. They've shot up today so I could make a killing. But I think I'll hold on to them. Do you think?

Weil Certainly. Certainly.

St Eglise Good. Good. Let's try our luck in the gaming room. Baccarat, I think. See if we're lucky there.

They go into the gaming room. Buller scribbles a note to Angel and hands it to him.

Buller (*to Lord Henry*) And how is Lord Henry this evening? Are you having a pleasant evening?

Lord Henry Leave me alone. Please.

Enter Marchese.

Marchese I would like a word with you.

Angel If you like.

Buller Then I'll join them at the table. (*Exit.*)

Marchese (*to Lord Henry*) You go too.

Angel What do you want? Have I offended you again?

Marchese Did you hear me?

Lord Henry leaves.

I have a proposition to make to you.

Angel How much do you want?

Marchese You have nothing left to give me.

Angel What makes you think that?

Marchese You're high and dry – you and your writer friend.

Angel If you want me you've no need to descend to threats.

Marchese I've told you already, how many times, that you are not my type. I haven't taken your money because I loved you. I loved you because you had money. You're getting old, but you must realise that. You've seen the competition. Not that you haven't got your qualities. But all you do now is ruin a man's nerves. Still, you're highly qualified for something I have in mind for you.

Angel Are you going to find me a job?

Marchese I told you I was an employment agent.

Angel I thought you were a police spy.

Marchese You can't make a living from that. I once helped a young man in need to find work in Valparaiso but he proved ungrateful and his father had me jailed for my troubles. But the authorities noticed my talent for intrigue and discretion and I did a deal. They give me a stipend of sorts. But it's only subsistence, so I resumed my former profession and I've shipped many a good-looking young fellow abroad to find work suited to his many natural talents.

Angel Life in such an establishment won't suit me. I haven't the talent for it. You can't imagine I could go with just anyone. Can you realise that I have an appetite for that kind of thing. That I can go with anyone.

Marchese In the Theopholous Oikonomopolous establishment in Cairo the clientele is hardly made up of anyone. Most of them come from the English aristocracy. But then there are the Turkish pashas and the Russian

diplomats, the Indian princes, and the Arab sheiks.
Then there are German industrialists. That kind of thing.
You've all the social talents required. You'll live in
apartments looking over the El Azhar mosque. You'll
dress as you please without any worry as to cost. Eat
well. Drink better. All the champagne you need. Your
clients will be rich men. And up to a point you'll have
your freedom. And if you really don't like a client there
are ways out, up to a point.

Angel Do you expect me to believe you when you say
your Egyptian friend will pay you thousands of francs
for someone he doesn't know from Adam?

Marchese I took the liberty of sending him some of your
pictures.

Angel The pictures I gave you.

Marchese (*pointing to Angel's portrait*) He'll hang that
one over his front door. And there's another advantage
to this opportunity. You'll be safe from those who have
an interest in your whereabouts – with Oikonomopolous
in Cairo. Certainly safer than you are here now.

Angel You must know I could never find myself in any
such place, no matter how amusing you made it sound.

Marchese Shall I whistle up the policeman, shall I?

Angel I can give you three thousand francs.

Marchese In Jungfrau shares. That's what your financial
position is. The public prosecutor pays in French francs
and Oikonomopolous pays in gold. I never deal in
shares. You could be in Cairo in a fortnight if you leave
tonight. Here things are so precarious for you. Beats me
how you haven't been picked up already. I found out
about you quickly enough. But I have a natural talent for
that. Still, I don't know how one of my colleagues hasn't
got on to you yet. I suppose it's only a matter of time.

The train leaves at half past midnight. We have to come to terms by eleven or I'll call the police.

Angel Are you serious about this?

Marchese My concern is only for your safety.

Angel I'll go anywhere with you. But I can't sell myself. It would be worse than prison. Have you no feelings for me?

Marchese Not feelings enough.

Angel I can't sell the only thing I can call my own. I'll give you everything we have.

Marchese I've had everything you've got in cash.

Angel I'll get Arthur to sell the shares.

Marchese No time. If we haven't left by eleven I'll have the pack of you deported in the morning. If we're going I must tell Hippolyte. Excuse me.

Arthur comes in from the gaming room.

Arthur I've hit a winning streak, Angel. Lord Henry is losing his shirt and Weil is betting in Jungfrau shares. Phillipeau isn't doing so badly. Aren't you coming in? (*Exits.*)

Angel Me in a brothel.

Angel reads Buller's note. Re-enter Arthur.

Arthur Won't you play?

Angel Why not? Why not? Get me a drink.

Arthur (*as they go*) I got *The Times* today. Hugo Anstruther has killed himself.

Angel stops. Arthur exits. Lord Henry comes in. Angel makes to go.

Lord Henry Am I so offensive to you?

Angel Good heavens, no. I have no time for you just now, that's all.

Lord Henry You never have time.

Angel No, I never do.

Lord Henry You've taken everything I have. I have given everything to you. I have nothing left. No life. Not a penny. You could at least try to be civil with me.

Angel And aren't I civil? What am I, then?

Lord Henry How can you be like this? What has happened to you? You have become quite quite quite hard. Have you forgotten our passionate exchanges when we were together in the hospital? You weren't so hard then. When I was ready to die for you.

Angel You gave me cholera. Have you forgotten that? It was your idea to give me cholera. That had a meaning, didn't it? What if I had died? Would that perhaps have suited you just as well? Really. Why are you so insistent in pursuing a fantasy that can't be realised? I said things then because of what the situation was then. Things have gone on.

Lord Henry It was deliberate. You knew what you were saying. Did you mean none of it? Was it all deceit?

Angel If you say so. In what way was it all deceit? Tell me. You have to be in this relation to me. You have to be. I have told you from the start that there is no way for you and me. Anyway. You have an admirer of your own now. Pick up with him.

Lord Henry I don't understand a word of what you're saying.

Angel Buller. Buller. Haven't you noticed? He's told me he's mad about you.

87

Lord Henry I don't envy you. I don't envy you at all. I only want you. I don't envy your terrible capacity for tormenting the weak nor your more terrible instinct for enslaving yourself to creatures of the night.

Angel Who do you mean in particular?

Lord Henry The Marchese. Who has vice emblazoned on his forehead like a sign.

Angel Be quiet before I kick you senseless. He loves me. When I look at him I realise how loathsome you are. If you don't want Buller why don't you try one of them in there? There are boys in there who do it for ready cash. If you have any left. Or shall I lend you some? Look at him. He'll do it for a glass of wine and a plate of oysters.

Lord Henry Do you think one day there will be a rebellion by people like me against people like you?

Angel Do you think one day there'll be a rebellion of people like me against people like you? You have a warm heart, Henry. I have something else. You had money, Henry. I had something else. Imagine having neither. There'd be cause for rebellion.

Enter Arthur, Buller, St Eglise, Weil, Baptiste, Hippolyte. Lord Henry goes out.

What has happened?

Arthur Nothing. I'm making money is what has happened. Come to supper.

Hippolyte Don't boast of winning at the tables. It's unlucky.

They exit. Buller keeps Angel back.

Buller Did you get my note?

Angel What I could understand of it. Go to the police if you must. Do you think I'm frightened of blackmail? I no longer have that kind of money.

88

Buller Don't lie to me, you lying bitch. You've still got twenty thousand in Jungfrau shares. Your fool of a writer friend has been boasting about it all night.

Angel Then go to him with your demands.

Buller It would take me two days to get him to grasp what I was talking about. And then I'd have to put up with his drivel about its relevance to art and what it brought to bear on what he's working on at the moment. I need cash.

Angel Why?

Buller I'm getting married, that's why. And don't laugh. I have had enough of this. I've met someone who's seen the man in me.

Angel Plenty of us have seen that.

Buller I mean someone who sees something in me. You'll think that's funny. You will. Your sort.

Angel Marry who you like. What do I care if you get married? You've been married before. But why have you been paying court to Henry Wantage?

Buller Because the man's an aristocrat. I know how useful such people can be. There's more than your sort. I'm after a bit of class. I'm not going to be a freak show again for anyone. Not used by anyone like you.

Angel You've got a little wife.

Buller Will you give me the money? I need it quick.

Angel I haven't got it and I don't give in to blackmail. It's Arthur's money.

Buller Then get him to sell up. He'll give you his last penny. Better get him to sell before he gambles it all away. He'll ruin himself, he's not careful.

89

Angel Always because of marriage. Marriage.

Buller You're not so smart. All you think about is him who's got hold of you. I know you. What does poor Arthur think of that?

Angel Do you want me to get him to show you out?

Buller Have it whichever way you like: if you haven't got the money for me by tomorrow it'll be the end of all this. I'll get some supper. (*Exit.*)

Angel I'm going to die of this.

Enter St Eglise.

St Eglise I'm looking for my young friend. Have you seen him? He's not at supper.

Angel No. No.

St Eglise Perhaps he's through here.

Going to the gaming room. Enter Weil.

Weil Have you . . . ?

Angel I think he's through there.

Enter Phillipeau.

Phillipeau Oh it's you. No. I . . .

Weil Through here.

Re-enter St Eglise.

St Eglise He's not there. Have you seen my young friend, either of you?

Phillipeau I haven't.

Weil Nor I. Perhaps he's at supper.

St Eglise No. Strange. Strange. (*Exit St Eglise.*)

Weil Poor old thing.

Phillipeau All of us. Aren't you going to have some supper?

Weil Go on without me.

Phillipeau Ha. Ha.

Weil No. No.

Angel and Phillipeau exit.

Poor old fools, all of us.

Enter Bob, wearing livery and holding a telegram.

Bob Are you Monsieur Weil, sir? They said I'd find you here.

Weil I am indeed.

Bob (*handing him the telegram*) For you, sir.

Weil (*reading*) 'Shares in the Jungfrau railway fallen to . . . ' Crashed. Well. Well. That's the way of things.

Bob Is that all, sir?

Weil Wait a minute. (*Tips him.*)

Bob Thank you, sir.

Weil What do they call you?

Bob My name's Lucien, sir, but they call me Bob.

Weil How old are you?

Bob Fifteen.

Weil Fifteen.

Weil exits. Enter August.

Bob Who are you, then. Eh?

August I'm hiding from them all. Have you seen St Eglise?

Bob No. They're all in there.

August I don't like it here. I wish I hadn't come.

Bob Come with me. Come downstairs. Come on.

August No.

Bob Yes. Come on. Come. No one'll find us down there. I'll show you. (*Kisses him.*)

    St Eglise enters.

St Eglise What's this? What's this, then?

    Re-enter Weil, Phillipeau and Lord Henry.

August I'm going. I'm going.

St Eglise I found him with a servant. You may laugh. Oh dear.

Weil You'd better sit down, I think.

St Eglise No. Darling. Baby. (*following August out*)

    The others go out, laughing.

Lord Henry Can't we play baccarat?

    Bob whispers to Angel. Lord Henry goes.

Angel Show him in.

    Bob opens the door to Slavin.

Slavin Where did you get him?

Angel From the circus.

Slavin What do you pay him?

Angel Ask him if you're so interested. Thank you. That will be all.

    Exit Bob.

Slavin I need some money, my dear.

Angel Do you?

Slavin I've taken an apartment for a lady friend and I'm short of the necessary.

Angel So you've got a lady friend, have you?

Slavin Yes. She's from Italy. She says she was married to the King of Naples, so she says. Something of a beauty in her time, if you can believe it.

Angel And you need the money badly.

Slavin She does – for the rent. Poor old girl. A lot to her, a trifle to you.

Angel Oh, God almighty. (*Laughs and breaks down.*)

Slavin There. There. Angel. What's this? I don't need it that bad. You ought to get some early nights, that's your trouble. That's right, you cry. I've seen you like this before, haven't I, eh? You could cry then, couldn't you? Bawl and shout, couldn't you, dear? Only then you didn't have shoes or such fine clothes, did you?

Angel Take me with you. Take me out of here, please.

Slavin I'll take you with me. We'll take a cab. But first tell me what it is, then. What's made you like this?

Angel They're going to hand me over to the police.

Slavin Who's going to hand you over to the police?

Angel The acrobat.

Slavin I'll see to him.

Angel Yes. Please. Please. Do for him. Do for him.

Slavin If he comes near me, that'll be the end of him. If he came to my lodgings, that would be the thing. My window opens onto the river. Only how can we get him there?

Angel Where do you live?

Slavin 376. Near the old Hippodrome, you know.

Angel I'll get him there. I'll get him there. Send me the rings he wears in his ears. I'd know then. You can take them off before you dispose of him. He don't notice when he's drunk.

Slavin And then?

Angel I'll give you the money. I'll get it. But are you sure?

Slavin Have I ever broken my word to you, ever?

Angel Off you go then. He'll be there. What is it?

Slavin How beautiful you still are. How you smell. How you smell. Let me. Let me. (*Kisses him.*) There we are. Payment. I could ask for more. You'd have to pay.

    Exit. Enter Buller.

Angel I think I have found a way out of our difficulty.

Buller Oh, have you then?

Angel Lord Henry is in a bad way. I'm afraid he may do something to himself and you may be the cause.

Buller What does he want?

Angel For you to take him away with you. He'll lend me two thousand pounds to save me from the police and if you'll take him with you I'll deposit the same amount in your name in any bank you name.

Buller And if I don't?

Angel Then you must turn me in. Arthur and I are destitute now, we are. Shall I call Lord Henry?

Buller I can't. My only interest in him is in connection with the aristocracy. He's taught me a few tricks of the trade. I'll give him that. No, I can't.

Angel He's waiting. What shall I say?

Buller My respects, but I'm not that hard up.

Angel I'll tell him then.

Buller No. Hang on. Hang on. I'll get two thousand pounds out of this, will I?

Angel Ask him yourself.

Buller I'm going into the dining room for a bowl of caviar and to get drunk first. (*He exits.*)

Angel calls Lord Henry. He enters.

Angel Henry. You have an opportunity to save me once more if you thought you could.

Lord Henry Have I? And how is that?

Angel By going to a house with Buller. He's threatened to denounce me to the police if you won't oblige him. You will oblige?

Lord Henry I couldn't. I couldn't. He'd be so brutal. I couldn't bear it. I couldn't. I can't.

Angel And what will happen to us all then, if he does as he says? There's a policeman on the corner.

Lord Henry I've got just enough for us to go steerage to America. You'd be safe enough there.

Angel No, you'll do this for me, won't you? America, I think not. Do you? You must tell him you can't do without him. Won't. Flatter him. You'll have to pay for the cab, by the way, here's the address. 376 rue Clairmont. They are expecting you.

Lord Henry Is this a test, is it?

Angel It is. It is. Please, Henry. It's a test.

Lord Henry Angel, you have so often deceived me, why should I believe you now?

Angel Because you do. Don't you? Do this for me. It's all vanity with him. And it flatters you in a way. I shall wait for you.

Lord Henry I cannot reconcile myself with your belief there is no God in heaven. And yet perhaps you're right and there's nothing in it. Let him come.

Angel Have you got the address?

Lord Henry Number 376. Yes.

Angel I'll wait for you. (*calling Buller*) Buller, darling.

Enter Buller.

Buller Excuse me, my mouth's full. Lord Henry.

Lord Henry Mr Buller. I beg you. I beg you. Mr Buller. I beg you.

Buller Yes. OK. You'll do. *À la lanterne.*

They both exit.

Angel Now for the other one. Bob. Bob.

Enter Bob.

Take off your livery.

Bob What sir?

Angel Change clothes with me. Where shall we go?

Bob Come this way.

Weil, Phillipeau, Arthur, August, St Eglise, Baptiste and Hippolyte rush in.

Phillipeau The scoundrel won't give me a chance to recoup.

Weil Your stake is worthless.

Phillipeau I have offered you my Jungfrau shares, sir.

Baptiste What is it?

Hippolyte Weil's taken all his money off him. And thrown in his hand.

Weil Who says that? I said I'll only play for cash. I'm not in the banking house now. And tomorrow, if he offered that trash to me in my office, it would be worth nothing.

Hippolyte What are these shares worth? What did you say?

Weil Yesterday they were worth so much it doesn't matter. Today they're worth nothing at all. Tomorrow, they'll do to line drawers.

Baptiste How has this happened?

Weil I've lost enough. Tomorrow I shall find I have lost everything. I'll start recovering from bankruptcy for the thirty-sixth time.

Arthur Is it true? The Jungfrau shares have fallen? We're ruined.

St Eglise Is this true, the Jungfrau shares have fallen?

Weil Fallen further than you ever thought. You poor old thing.

St Eglise Oh my God. My fortune. (*Collapses.*)

August Dear God.

Arthur and August minister to St Eglise.

Baptiste Dear God.

Hippolyte Let us go, it's getting unpleasant here. Jew. Can't be trusted, you see.

They exit, leaving Arthur, August, St Eglise and Weil.

Arthur Get him a drink.

August Yes. (*Gets him a drink.*)

Arthur You'll feel better now.

Weil I'm sorry, old chap. But that's playing the market. (*Exits.*)

August brings a drink.

August Come on now, old thing.

Angel enters wearing livery.

Angel Have you any cash, Arthur?

Arthur Are you mad? Didn't you hear?

Angel Well then, in two minutes they will be here. We'll be sold. We could have got a cab. Stay if you want to.

Arthur No. We'd better go, I think.

August Come on, old chap.

St Eglise What shall I do?

August Come on. Come on.

Police whistle. Police chase involving all those who have recently left. They arrest Bob.

Policeman Got you.

Marchese You have arrested the wrong man.

SEVEN

*London. An attic room divided to provide accommodation
for Angel, Arthur and Slavin. There is a curtain leading
to Angel's quarters, a makeshift partition making a small
dwelling for Slavin, and the principle space where Arthur
is lying on a mattress covered with a blanket. Angel is
walking about trying to keep warm. Slavin is seated,
drinking from an old cup with a jug beside him.*

Arthur Listen to the rain.

Angel Feel the cold.

Slavin Have a drop of this, then, why don't you. No?
It won't warm you up but it'll make you feel better. No?
Gin takes people in different ways. Makes some people
very sorry for themselves. Not me. Not me. Pint of gin,
I got it downstairs. She's got a nice little gin shop.
Down there. Nice fire. She's an enterprising woman.
She likes me so she must be enterprising. She got a notice
up: 'Drunk a penny, dead drunk for tuppence.' She's a
proper businesswoman and knows how to make a thing
attractive. I'm going down later when I've got through
this. Only I ain't got no money. She'll let me have a
warm.

Angel (*looking into a bowl which is catching water from
the ceiling*) This bowl is full. What shall I do?

Slavin Chuck it out the window.

Angel does.

Angel I think the rain's stopped.

Slavin Well, now's the time, if you're going to do it.
The clerks in the city will still be going home. You'll miss
out, you wait much longer. What's stopping you?

Angel No.

Arthur No. I don't want you to.

Angel Oh, don't you? You can afford principles now, can you?

Arthur Don't, Angel. I'm ill.

Angel If I had decent clothes, I'd go up west.

Slavin No. You're better home here. They won't shop you over here. They might rob you. But they won't shop you. Up west they'll rob you and shop you. They're more morally progressive.

Angel I wish I was dead.

Arthur Let's just lie here and let's try to sleep. Let's not be angry any more. And let's hope we never wake up.

Angel Shut up, Arthur. Don't philosophise now, for Jesus Christ's sake.

They hear the sound of a band playing 'God Rest Ye Merry Gentlemen'.

Arthur Is it Christmas?

Slavin It's good to be home at Christmas.

Angel Why don't you get up and try to find work?

Arthur Because I'm ill.

Slavin He's not well.

Angel Let me get in with you. I'm so cold. I got to get warm somehow.

Angel gets under the blanket with Arthur.

Give me a drink.

Slavin Certainly. Certainly.

Arthur and Angel both have a drink.

It's a cure-all. It'll cheer you up and keep his fever down.

Angel It's the quickest way out of here, anyway. Though Arthur's poems would do the trick just as well.

Slavin Yes. It's a universal benefit. From the cradle to the grave. The old girl's got a handle on social policy.

Arthur I wish we were in Paris dining at Maxim's.

Slavin A slice of Christmas pudding'd do for me. I think she'll keep me some – her downstairs.

Arthur I've been dreaming of the perfect cigarette.

Angel Shut up. Shut up.

Arthur I'm ill.

Angel I know you're ill. Don't go on about it. What can I do?

Arthur And you made me ill. I got this from you.

Angel I'm not ill. I'm just freezing cold.

Arthur You got infected by your Parisian pimp.

Angel Don't blame me. You've got nothing from me, ever. Ever. I saw you with who you got it from. And I thought you believed in faith, fidelity, whatever you like to call it. I'm going out.

Arthur No, stay here. I've tried to get a job. I thought I had a perfect system with numbers. But I don't have the cash. I've tried it with rich women. But my clothes were too shabby. And they want a presentable escort.

Slavin I'd have thought you'd have done well with women. You've got a bit of tone.

Angel He'd bore them by talking about art.

Slavin No, women like you to talk. They like a bit of conversation. Women – they're not so crude as men in many ways. Many ways. A woman likes a laugh. Likes a bit of attention. Likes you to like 'em. I like women. She likes to hear your opinions. No – Arthur was unlucky there.

Angel What are we going to do?

Slavin I've given my advice. I've given my advice.

Arthur I don't want you to.

Angel I shall have to.

Arthur I forbid you to.

Angel Lie down, Arthur. I'm going out. Give me my shoes. Put some paper in them.

   Slavin does so.

We haven't got a mirror.

Slavin You look all right. Come here. You look a picture. Listen to me. Don't be frightened. It's always alarming the first time and a little bit exciting, eh? But bring 'em back here. We can keep an eye open for you here. Here, eat one of these. (*giving him a sweet*) Take the smell of gin off your breath.

Arthur I want none of the money.

Angel You'll want it when I get it. (*Angel exits.*)

Slavin We'll go there – he brings anybody back. If he brings anybody back.

Arthur I've known him since we were children. It's as if we were brothers. I remember Dr Goulderie calling to see how my mother was. He was about fifteen. He couldn't take his eyes off him, the good doctor. Angel bought him my first book of poems. He's always been like a bright intelligent superior child. When he was a child he was always interested in my work. Listened to me play on the piano. Liked me to explain things. I watched him go from my father to Goulderie, to the artist, to my father, who was always possessive of him, and who he always betrayed – eventually with me. After he shot him. Who knows how the world works. There was always a closeness between us then. I didn't understand – that's why he had such power over me.

Slavin Sh. Hang on. *(listening)*

Arthur What?

Slavin Hang . . . Yes . . .

Arthur I can't bear it. I'll throw him out.

Slavin You haven't got the strength for such a thing. Come on, up you get. Let's get you in there. Quiet now.

Arthur I can't bear it. I don't want to hear.

Slavin You've heard it before.

They hide behind the partition. Enter Angel with Tomkins.

Angel It's not much.

Tomkins puts his fingers to his mouth.

It's cold. There's no fire.

Tomkins puts his hand over Angel's mouth.

What do you mean?

Tomkins puts his hand over Angel's mouth and a finger to his own lips.

I don't know what you mean. You'd better go, I think. You're all right. No one can hear us.

We can see Arthur and Slavin. Tomkins still indicates silence.

I've never done this. I've never been with anyone I haven't been introduced to or whose name I didn't know. Do you believe me? No, I bet you don't. I don't know what to say.

Tomkins makes another silencing motion.

Yes. It's never interested me. Things that must be quite exciting, I should think. It's true. I missed out on a lot. What do you like? Do you take it, all that?

Tomkins comes towards Angel.

What?

Tomkins tries to kiss him.

No. Don't kiss me. You're not supposed to kiss. No, I can't be like that.

Kisses him.

I hope you've got some money.

Tomkins hands him money. Angel inspects it. Tomkins takes it back. He holds Angel's mouth shut as a signal to be quiet.

All right.

Takes the lamp and leads him behind the curtain.

Arthur What's happened?

Slavin Sh.

Arthur You can't hear anything from here.

Slavin I've heard it too many times.

Arthur I've got to listen.

Slavin goes through his pockets. Arthur listens at the curtain.

Slavin Nothing but a pair of gloves. What's this? (*Reads a pamphlet.*) 'Exhortations to pious men and those with the intention of becoming so.' Very helpful. Two-and-sixpence. Come on, let's go back. Come on.

They go behind the partition. Angel and Tomkins come out.

Angel Well then. Do you want to do it again?

Tomkins holds Angel's mouth shut. He puts his coat on, gives Angel the pamphlet. Refuses Angel's offer to take him to the door. Arthur and Slavin come out.

Arthur How much did he give you?

Angel Here it is. Take it. Go on. I'm going out again.

Slavin Sh. He's coming back.

Arthur He's coming for his prayer book.

Angel It isn't him. It's someone else. Who is it?

Slavin Some acquaintance of his who has recommended us to him.

Laughs. Enter Lord Henry, poorly dressed and carrying a rolled-up canvas.

Lord Henry If I've come at an inconvenient time, I'll go. But I haven't spoken to anyone for ten days now. I think I ought to tell you that I couldn't get any money. My brother didn't reply.

Slavin So now you'd like to get your legs under our table, is that it, my lord?

Angel I'm going out.

Lord Henry I haven't come entirely empty-handed. Look: on my way here I was offered ten shillings for it in a junk shop. But I couldn't part with it.

Slavin What is it, then?

Angel Show us.

Arthur takes the canvas and unrolls it.

Arthur Look, it's Angel's portrait.

Angel And you've brought it here, did you, you . . . (*screaming*) Get rid of it. Get rid of it. I don't want to see it.

Arthur What's wrong with you? Look at it. Just to look at it again makes me understand why what's happened has happened. Look at him. Look. Let anyone who looks at that tell me what he would have done.

Slavin Yes, he's a good-looking boy. We must find a nail for it. It will impress the customers.

Arthur There's one over here.

Slavin How did you acquire it?

Lord Henry That night in Paris. I cut it out of the wall.

Slavin Pity it's so damaged. You should have been more careful with it. You'll need a nail at the bottom, too.

Arthur I know what I'm doing. (*Nails the picture to the wall with his boot.*) There.

Slavin It gives the place an air of luxury already.

Arthur looks at it.

Arthur Look. Look.

Slavin Yes. Yes.

Lord Henry Who painted it, did you say?

Arthur Didn't you know him?

Lord Henry Only that he cut his throat and that you despised him. He was very talented.

Angel I'm going out again.

Arthur (*still looking*) In spite of everything, he's still the same. The same look in the eyes. But you've aged, Angel. I hadn't noticed.

Slavin The bloom gone. Ah yes. But you can still say . . . that's the thing about a painting – you can still say that's what I used to look like. No one you pick up tonight will have any idea of our glory days, eh? They won't believe it.

Arthur One doesn't notice the change when you're with someone every day.

Slavin Still, down there he's still worth a dozen of them. Aren't you? Anyway, what matters out there are qualities of the heart. You look for the eyes which are least likely to rob you.

Angel makes to go.

Arthur You're not going down there again. Not while I've got a breath in me.

Lord Henry Where are you going?

Arthur He's going to pick someone up and bring them up here. He's had one already.

Lord Henry I'll come with you, Angel. I'll come with you.

Slavin Here, not on his patch.

Lord Henry I'll be near. I'll look after you.

Angel You're all killing me.

Angel exits, followed by Lord Henry.

Arthur This is hopeless. Hopeless.

Slavin We should have stopped that Lord Henry fellow. He'll frighten 'em off. Look of him'd be enough to put anyone off his stroke. Still, you've got to give it to him.

If he hadn't brought the big fellow to my place in Paris, we'd still have him hanging around today.

Arthur My life. It's been utterly useless. Utterly. Utterly. I'm useless.

Slavin The lamp's going out. There's no oil either. It's getting dark.

Arthur My life. Where is it? Where has it gone? He's taken my life. (*Listens.*)

Slavin Hey. Hey. Yes. Yes. We're in luck. Come on.

> *They go behind the partition. Enter Angel with Euba. The first words heard outside the door.*

Euba It's dark. Where's the light?

Angel Come on. Come on. It's all right.

Euba Why is it so dark?

Angel The lamp has gone out. Come on. Come. It's all right.

Euba And it's cold.

Angel Do you want a drink?

Euba Yes, give me a drink.

> *Angel gives him some gin.*

Good.

Slavin (*from behind the partition*) Blimey, it's a Shwarzer. That's a turn up. Still. What's up with you, Arthur? Did you think this was really the occupation of passionate refinement like yours? Do you think they don't do it or something? Or do you think it's a result of oppression? Only natural in people like you. Sex isn't prejudiced, Arthur. It's the true colonist. It pitches its tent in all of us. And we all have our different tasks to perform. Now, me, I'm different to you. But I suspect, Arthur, things

might have been different for you if it hadn
Angel. You'd have fell for some girl in the cho
way out. I only did it when it was sometimes a
Well, it's all a necessity, ain't it? We're in Whitecha
Arthur. The hub of the Empire. We're not in Kensing
Square.

Angel More? No. You're beautiful, aren't you?

Euba goes to kiss Angel.

Hang on, have you got any money?

Euba I've got a gold sovereign.

Angel Let's see it.

Euba I'll give it to you.

Angel I must see it.

Euba You'll see it.

Angel No – now.

Euba shows him the sovereign. He kisses but doesn't give him the money.

Euba I never pay before. You'll get it later. You will.

Grabs him. Angel moves away.

Angel Stop it. Get off. Stop it.

Euba You'll get it, I swear.

Angel Get off.

Enter Arthur.

Arthur Leave him alone.

Euba Who are you? Why you got him here? (*Hits Arthur savagely on the head with a cosh.*) That's right, boy. Sleep. (*to Angel*) Why did you do that? I would have paid you. (*Goes.*)

Slavin comes out.

Angel Arthur. Look here. Look at him. You see to him. I'm going out. I'm going out again. (*Angel exits.*)

Slavin He can't take it. He'll never make a living out of love because love is his life. Come on, Arthur. Blood! Arthur. Oh dear. Well, you can't stay here. I'll put you in there, otherwise you'll put the customers off. Come on, up you get. No. He's gone. Well. Come on. (*He drags him behind the partition.*) No. Leave him in peace, eh. I'd better be leaving then. I think I'll go downstairs, see if she's got a bit of Christmas pudding for me.

On his way out he meets Lord Henry.

You going to make your quarters here, then? Just see none of the valuables are pinched, OK?

Lord Henry It's dark.

Slavin Yes. Arthur's in there. He's retired for the evening. I wouldn't disturb him. If anyone wants me, I'm downstairs having a drink with a friend. (*to the audience*) I'm going now, you'll pick up the rest. There's not a lot I can do.

Lord Henry I'll watch him do it with strangers as I've watched him with all the others. It's my punishment. Only someone who is not human like I am, not human, can watch how much they don't understand themselves, all these people. That everything they do is senseless and everything they say is false. Today one thing, tomorrow another, according to what they've eaten, drunk or made love or perhaps none of these things. The children are intelligent but they grow into animals. And no one knows what he's doing. When they're hungry, they don't have time to be unhappy, and when they're full, they make the world an atrocity, and then they act entirely by whim. I wonder if anyone has ever been made happy by love. That's what my fate is – not to know. I'm not human. I thank God for that. But I seem to have human capacity. I'd better hang myself. If I was drowning in my own blood I don't think he'd care even then. He has always hated me and I don't know why. Why are men so terrible to men? I've been useful to him. There is that. I could jump off the bridge. The water under the bridge is colder than his heart. I could dream until I drowned. I could dream he was kissing me, as I often dream it. But I always wake again. Ah, yes. The Thames for all its filth is far too clean for me.

He tries to hang himself. The chair gives way but the rope breaks.

I must still bear this life. Oh God, whisper in his ear. Tell him to love me. Love me, please. Love me. Listen to him. Let me be happy just once. Just once. My angel, my star, my love. Pity me. Pity me. Pity me.

Enter Angel with Jack.

Jack Who's that?

Angel It's no one, it's my brother. He's demented. He's ill. Take no notice of him.

Lord Henry Is that you?

Angel Yes. Be quiet.

Jack You've got a pretty mouth on you.

Angel So they tell me. I haven't had any complaints.

Jack No. How much do you want? I haven't got a lot.

Angel Are you going to stay the night?

Jack Why do you ask that? I can't. I got to get back.

Angel You can go home in the morning. Say you missed the omnibus. Stayed with a friend.

Jack How much do you want?

Angel I don't want a lot. What have you got?

Jack No. I'm off. I'm off.

Angel No, please stay. Please. Please. Please.

Jack What do you want me to stay all night for? What you up to, eh? What you going to do when I'm asleep?

Angel Nothing. Don't be afraid.

Jack I'm not afraid.

Angel Don't go, please.

Jack How much do you want, then?

Angel Half of what we said in the street.

Jack Too much. You haven't been doing this long, have you?

Angel The first time tonight.

Lord Henry Angel.

Angel Get out.

Jack He's not your brother, is he? What you got here. He's in love with you, isn't he? Poor creature. (*stroking Lord Henry's head*) Go on. Go on.

Angel Why are you looking at me like that?

Jack I'm looking at you. That's all. You'll be better stripped, eh? I thought that in the street. And your mouth's pretty. I've only got this. (*Takes a coin out.*)

Angel It doesn't matter. Give it to me.

Jack You'll have to split it. I'll need my fare in the morning.

Angel I haven't got any money.

Jack Turn your pockets out.

Angel I've got this. (*Shows his empty hand.*) That's all I've got.

Jack Give it back.

Angel I'll get change in the morning.

Jack No, give it here. Come on.

Angel All right. Come on. I'll light the lamp.

Jack We don't need light. The moonlight'll be enough.

Angel I like you. I do.

They go behind the curtain.

Lord Henry I must go home. I mustn't stay here. I can't. They'll forgive me. I'll finish my degree. I'll do what they say.

Angel (*off*) No, stop. Don't. You're hurting.

Jack You want me to.

Angel No.

Jack Yes.

Angel, partly dressed, comes right out followed by Jack. Lord Henry aims his revolver at Jack. Jack stabs him in the stomach.

(*to Lord Henry*) You be quiet now. (*to Angel*) Now then, what's your pretty mouth for?

There's a very bitter struggle during which Angel tries to bottle Jack. Eventually Jack controls him with his knife.

Angel No. Please. No. Please. No.

Jack Shut it. Shut up. Shut up.

Jack pushes Angel over the table and fucks him violently, threatening him all the time with the knife.

Angel No. No. No. No.

Jack Yes. Yes. Yes.

Angel continues to say 'No' until Jack forces him to say 'Yes' with the knife. Angel eventually cries out 'No.' Jack cuts his throat. He throws Angel onto the floor.

(*recovering*) Yeah. That was good. That was good. (*Washes his hands in the basin, which has been collecting water.*) No towel. (*He uses Lord Henry's scarf. To Lord Henry*) Don't be frightened. I'm not interested in you. You won't be long yet anyway. (*He goes.*)

Lord Henry Where are you? Where are you? My dearest. Let me see you. Angel, my angel. I'll stay with you through eternity. Oh God, help me.

The End.